The Replication of the Father Serra Statue

A Community Volunteer Project

by

Catherine Antolino Mervyn

Edited by

Terry Ruscin—William Mervyn

Cover Design by

Terry Ruscin—Sandi Whitaker

ISBN: 1-4033-0986-8 (e-book)
ISBN: 1-4033-0987-6 (Paperback)
ISBN: 1-4033-0988-4 (Hardcover)

This book is printed on acid free paper.

1stBooks - rev. 10/15/02

www.ingramcontent.com/pod-product-compliance
Lightning Source LLC
Chambersburg PA
CBHW022113170526
45157CB00004B/1622

ACKNOWLEDGEMENTS

Mrs. Mervyn is deeply indebted first to Bill, her husband, devoted editor and mentor, to Shirley Weeks, Carol Green, Richard Newsham, Russell Burns, Wilbur Rubottom, Jim Monahan of Ventura, and Judy Monzo of Camarillo. Each provided important information; all were part of this historical project. Additionally, the author is most grateful to Terry Ruscin, author-photographer for much general encouragement in the preparing this manuscript for publication and the cover design, and to Don Mills for the use of his photo of the Serra Statue dedication.

Finally, Mrs. Mervyn is also indebted to Jeff Maulhardt, author and former student of hers, for his support, and for providing special photos which have enhanced this work.

TABLE OF CONTENTS

FROM THE AUTHOR

The state of California proudly displays, in various locations, a variety of statues of the Franciscan priest, Father Junípero Serra, founder of nine of California's 21 historic missions. Only the city of San Buenaventura, however, can boast of three similar statues, one of concrete, one of wood, and one of bronze. This is the story of how these three statues grew out of the heart of the people of the "City by the Sea."

TO THEM THIS STORY IS DEDICATED

November 1992

PREFACE

"To our knowledge no one has ever attempted to replicate a sculpture in this manner from stone [concrete] to wood to bronze."

The above inscription can be seen on the San Buenaventura Jaycee plaque placed at the base of the nine-foot-four-inch woodcarving of Father Junípero Serra in the atrium of the San Buenaventura, California City Hall in the year 1989.

What was it that enabled a group of carvers from the Channel Island Woodcarvers Association to achieve what had never been achieved before?

To contemplate the impressive wooden form and feel the powerful strength that exudes from it is to sense for a fleeting moment what may have inspired the monumental task of replicating a statue from concrete to wood to bronze.

Catherine Antolino Mervyn

FOREWORD

Fray Junípero Serra's bronze effigy stands, in various forms, at Statuary Hall in Washington, D.C., San Francisco's Golden Gate Park, The "Old Plaza" in Los Angeles, and San Fernando Valley's Brand Park. A "life-sized" (five-foot, two-inch) casting from a common mold stands at each of California's historic Spanish missions. Still others inspire homage in the Balearic Island of Mallorca, Serra's birthplace. And there are more, though perhaps the most striking of the memorials rises proudly from a pedestal fronting City Hall at San Buenaventura.

Junípero Serra, O.F.M. (1713-1784) was a Mallorcan priest and missionary, California's first European citizen, and a stalwart visionary devoted to indoctrinating indigenous peoples with the principles of Christianity. His legacy included California's 21 missions—the first nine having been founded under his administration as *presidente* of the spiritual conquest. Known later as the "Apostle of California," Serra was beatified in 1988 and aficionados eagerly anticipate his canonization. It is only fitting that several artisans have fashioned for public display what they believe to be seemly representations of this truly amazing eighteenth-century pioneer.

The nine-foot, four-inch sculpture at San Buenaventura perhaps best captures the powerful essence of Serra, the man whose motto was *"siempre adelante, nunca atrás"* ("always go forward and never turn back"). The bronze statue fronting City Hall today is, moreover, the second iteration of the original concrete form. The interim sculpture was fashioned from basswood.

An elaborate historical account of the three statues at San Buenaventura is chronicled meticulously in this treatise by Catherine Antolino Mervyn, herself a European immigrant. Concetta Antolino arrived from Italy on Ellis Island at the tender age of 13 and in California attained the American Dream with her career as educator and avocation as author. She shares in common with *Fray* Junípero Serra his *"siempre adelante"* adage in life's tasks and challenges and counts herself among his advocators. It is most relevant that she has assembled this history—of a memorial to a fellow immigrant—as a testimony to the rich cultural heritage of the Golden State and its founding father.

Terry Ruscin

Author, Photographer, Historian

July 16, 2001

INTRODUCTION

JUNÍPERO SERRA

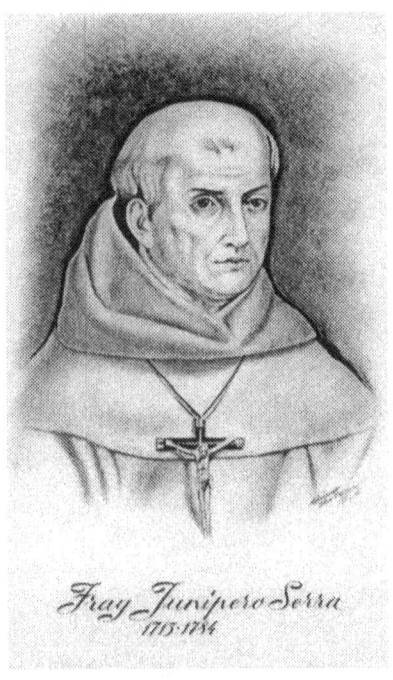

The enduring prevalence of California's historic missions is due mainly to the love and dedication of one man, the "Apostle of California."

Volumes have been written about the Franciscan priest, Junípero Serra (1713-1784)—the most celebrated missionary who helped settle California.

Known as the founder of the California missions, Serra's likeness can be found in the most unlikely places, from the magnificence of Statuary Hall at the national Capitol Building, Washington, D.C. to the humbleness of a second-hand store window on Santa Barbara's trendy State Street. One can even perhaps venture 30 miles south of there to the city of Ventura where Father Serra is honored as the city's founder, and may find three nine-foot statues of him.

Artists have interpreted Serra in many forms and media from the most ordinary to the most precious, paralleling his own life from the farming fields of Mallorca in the Balearic Isles, to beatification in the Catholic Church.

The journey, however, from one level to the other was not light or effortless; the struggles he met were many and arduous.

Serra was born in 1713 in Petra on the island of Mallorca. Early in his youth he entered the Franciscan Order of Friars Minor. He rose to the status of professor at the Lullian University in Palma where he achieved renown as a man of profound learning, as well as a great teacher and orator.

In 1750, however, Serra's long-time desire to become a missionary was finally fulfilled and he, along with a group of his student-disciples, was sent to the Sierra Gorda in

Mexico as missionary. There he spent nine years in which he demonstrated remarkable qualities as a spiritual leader and builder of missions.

In 1767, when Franciscans were sent to Lower California, Serra was sent as their *Presidente.*

He had scarcely established his friars in the lower peninsula when colonial Spain moved its boundaries north to occupy Upper California. Explorer Portolá led the colonists while Serra and his disciples carried the Gospel to his beloved Indians.

In Upper California Serra established the first mission at San Diego, but made his home at Monterey where he established a second mission, and called it San Carlos Borromeo.

While president of the California missions, Serra devoted his life to the welfare of the California Indians, and established the first nine of the present-day 21 missions, beginning with Mission San Diego and concluding with Mission San Buenaventura.

Many of California's cities bear the names of missions that were founded in their locations. The official name of San Buenaventura was shortened to Ventura in the early days of the railroad when the longer name could not fit into the train schedules. However, the longer name remains and is used in official records.

Serra happily wore the well known Franciscan habit for the remainder of his days, went home to God on August 28, 1784, and was buried the next day at Mission San Carlos in Carmel, California.

Anyone searching for a model to follow as an example of an untiring, courageous and spiritual leader, can well delve into the many books on the life of Father Junípero Serra, the "Gentle Giant," to find inspiration.

Catherine Antolino Mervyn

THE CONCRETE STATUE

The 1930s were the years of the Great Depression.
America saw nearly twelve million of her people out of
work. Over five thousand banks closed and business was at
a standstill.

In 1933 the newly elected President, Franklin D. Roosevelt, pledged a "New Deal" for the American people. Soon after his inauguration, steps were taken to give the nation relief from unemployment. A number of public works programs were instituted, and people memorized their acronyms as if they were prayers or famous words.

For needy young men there was the Civilian Conservation Corps (CCC) which provided work in national parks, and the National Youth Administration (NYA) which established classes where trades and professions could be learned. Part-time jobs were found for many students, making it possible for them to continue on to more advanced studies.

To help farmers there was the Agricultural Adjustment Act (AAA), and the National Recovery Act (NRA) for Business and Industry.

In 1935 there were still more than eleven million people out of work. In that year the Works Progress Administration (WPA) became the chief relief agency of the government. It provided employment for a wide variety of people including skilled craftsmen, unemployed actors, writers, musicians, artists, and members of other professions.[1]

It was at such a time of national crisis that John Palo Kangas, the sculptor, was commissioned by the Works Progress Administration (WPA) and the County of Ventura to create a statue of the legendary Franciscan missionary, Father Junípero Serra, the founder of the first nine of California's 21 historic missions. Kangas, grateful for the appointment, began his work in earnest in his Los Angeles studio.

Anxious to know his subject intimately, the artist made many visits to Santa Barbara and San Buenaventura missions, consulting with priests and other religious who knew of Serra's life and work.

Moreover, Kangas felt the need to know Serra as a human being, sensitive to other human beings.

Serra was born of poor farming parents on the Island of Mallorca, off the coast of Spain. While at home he was often plagued with minor illnesses. Despite the delicacy of his early youth, however, Serra had a character that was strong and vigorous. Timothy Cardinal Manning spoke of him as "the ox, harnessed to the plough."

Kangas did not seem overly concerned about Serra's physical appearance. Some writers say that Serra was a small man, 5′2" or 3" at best, while Kangas finally formed a 9′4" concrete giant.[2]

According to J. Paul Morgan, a contemporary of the artist and former coach and principal at Cabrillo Junior High School, San Buenaventura, Kangas was elated one day when he saw a man who resembled the "Serra" he had visualized in stature as well as facial structure. His name was Gordon Douglas of Meiners Oaks, California, a small village near the city of San Buenaventura.[3]

The artist's pencil flew deftly across the blank pages. There emerged a vital, energetic human form, that of a man who could endure pain and experience love. The missionary figure Kangas drew had a powerful jaw and a purposeful forward-looking vision, reflective of the motto the missionary would embrace, *"Siempre adelante, nunca atrás!"* ("Always go forward, never turn back!")

The cassock of a Franciscan priest covered his body and a heavy cincture encircled his waist. In one hand he held a book, the priestly breviary, in the other a staff which told the story of his painful walks on an ulcerated leg from one mission to the other along the desolate California coast. The drawings Kangas made in his Los Angeles studio were in preparation for the creation of the Serra symbol. The Finnish-born sculptor was eager to sculpt a great work of art.

The Serra statue was to be made of concrete, undoubtedly the most economical medium in those days of national gloom.

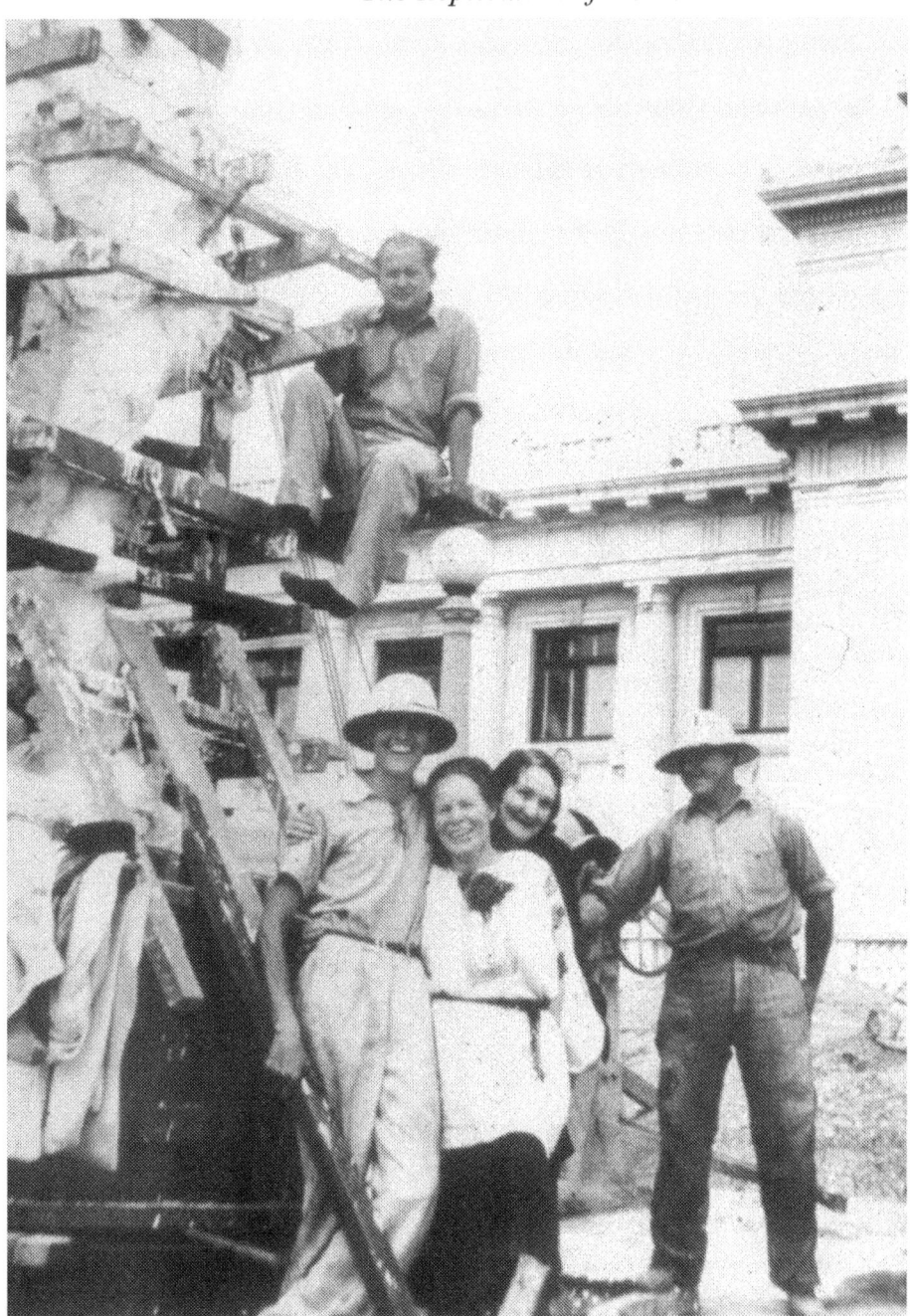

Artist John Paul Kangas—Pouring of concrete for original statue

Kangas first sculpted a scale clay model which he used as a guide in building a full-size clay pattern—"a larger than life-size statue of a friar…"[4]

To make the huge pattern, he first built a full-size armature or frame-work of wood and chicken wire, as is done with papier-mache. He then covered the framework with layers of clay. By the use of special calipers and other measuring instruments, he compared the full-size pattern with the scale model. Over the pattern Kangas built a mold of plaster-of-Paris, which gave him a reverse hollow mold known as a break-away mold.

The break-away, or reverse, mold was taken to San Buenaventura and placed on an imposing permanent location in front of the County Courthouse overlooking the ocean.

A strong protective scaffold was built around the entire hollow mold to keep it from breaking, and wet concrete was poured into it, right on location. When it hardened, the break-away mold was removed and some final smoothing was done.[5]

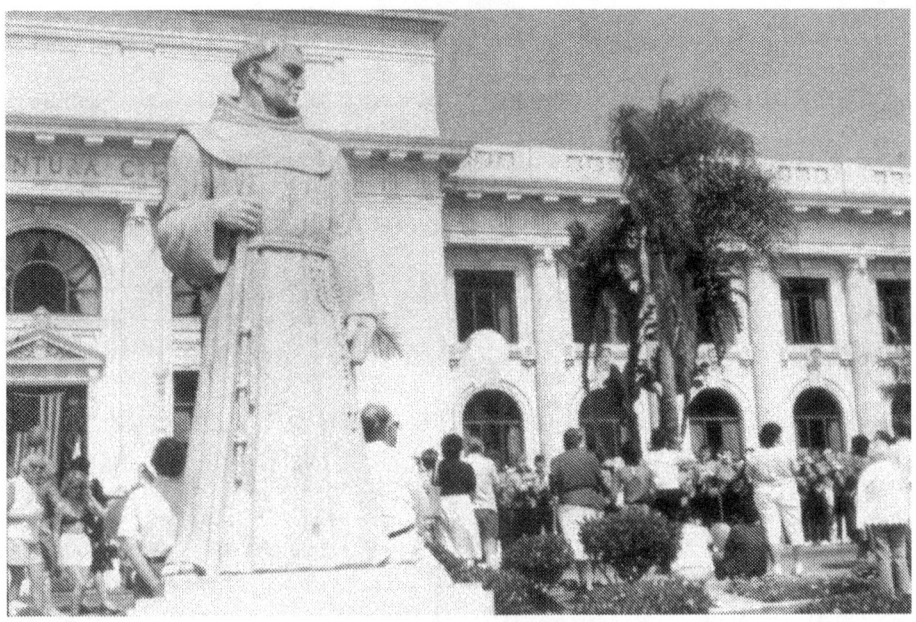

Serra concrete statue

Dedication ceremonies were held in November 1937, and were led by Governor Frank F. Merriam who paid homage to the "beloved Father of the Missions." Father Maynard J. Geiger, a Franciscan Serra biographer was present, as was Adolpho Ortega who did the unveiling.

Ortega was a descendant of Captain Francisco Ortega, a Serra contemporary. After 155 years, Serra once again looked out toward the sea and the California coast. The location became a favorite gathering place for fiestas, weddings, and a variety of social affairs.

Many respected historians have written about Serra's compassionate work among the native Indians of Mexico and California. He is known and revered from his native Spain to Mexico and the United States. His likeness in Statuary Hall, Washington, D.C. is witness to the honor given him by Californians. He lived to found nine of California's 21 historic missions.

The first was mission San Diego de Alcalá, now the great metropolis of San Diego. Next was San Carlos Borromeo del Río Carmelo, known as the Carmel Mission on the shores of Monterey Bay, where Serra is buried. San Antonio de Padua followed, then San Gabriel Arcángel, San Luis Obispo, San Francisco de Asís, San Juan Capistrano, and Santa Clara de Asís. The last to see Serra's imprint was San Buenaventura, where he is revered as the founder of the city that bears the mission's name.

The name "Ventura" is an abbreviated form of the name San Buenaventura. History tells that the original name was too long for use on the early train schedules; therefore it was shortened to "Ventura". In 1969, however, Councilwoman Barbara Udsen moved that the name, "San Buenaventura" be used on all official correspondence; the motion passed unanimously.[6] Today all city official documents bear the mission's illustrious name.

Catherine Antolino Mervyn
CASTING THE CONCRETE STATUE

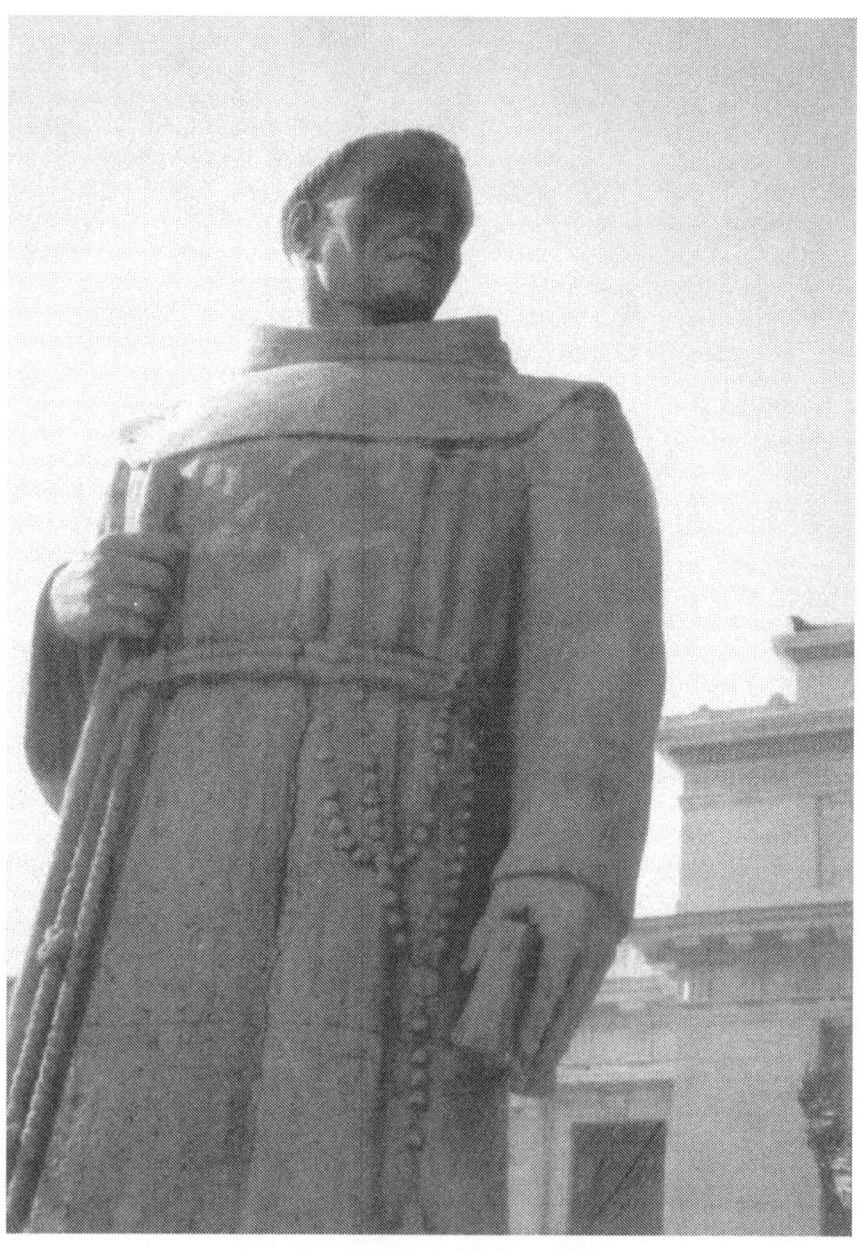

Concrete statue showing deterioration—circa 1980s

Kangas, the artist, died in 1958 in Los Angeles. Meanwhile the old building, the Ventura County Courthouse—which for 50 years had served as background for Kangas' "reactive concrete" master-piece—had outgrown the increased population, was ultimately condemned.

In 1971 the County Government Offices were moved to new, larger quarters. The city of San Buenaventura then purchased the old courthouse from the county and restored it. The neo-classic State Historic Landmark #487, built in 1912, became the new stately San Buenaventura City Hall.

The concrete Serra statue that stood in front of the venerable building was part of the purchase.[7] Years of sea-air weathering were not kind to the noble Serra concrete monument, nor were vandals of the 60s and 70s who sought release of their pent-up energies by defacing the statue with spray paint. Interested citizens of San Buenaventura began to vent their frustration in the City Council Chambers; they found it demoralizing to see the deterioration and vandalism that was destroying their beloved historic symbol, which for years had held a prominent place in the Ventura County Seal as well as in the City's Seal.[8]

The County Board of Supervisors had been made aware of the effect of sea air on "reactive concrete" in a study of the Matilija Dam, also built of "reactive concrete." The dam was ultimately condemned. There was speculation among them and city officials as to whether the same mixture might have been used in the Serra statue.[9]

For 51 years the concrete symbol had stood in front of the old courthouse. It was a historical landmark affirming the history of the city's origin.

As early as 1983, Councilman Russell Burns, a mechanical engineer by profession, had presented a report to the City Council in which he stated: "The [Serra] statue, 9'4" in height, was sculpted in clay and cast in concrete. Unfortunately, the aggregate used in the concrete mixture, combined with salt air, has deteriorated the concrete, and as a result the statue is cracking and in the not too distant future will fall apart."[10]

Burns followed his report with a recommendation for "some treatment of the concrete" which would slow down the action. However, he also reaffirmed that eventually the statue would disintegrate.[11]

Shortly thereafter, the city commissioned three studies of the statue—one by an art conservator, a second by an engineering firm, and a third by a concrete expert—in order to plan the best way to preserve it. By June of 1984 the results of all the studies agreed that the statue should be moved inside. Relocating, however, would only "arrest deterioration," they explained. The statue was too fragile and worn to be copied by latex molding. Made of "reactive" or "wet" concrete aggregate, the statue had expanded and developed deep fissures. The studies determined that the concrete would continue to react to the sea air. Additionally, sandblasting the vandals' paint had destroyed the statue's original splendor. Spraying it would not prevent further damage. The choice path to follow would be to have a more durable statue, one of bronze.[12]

Councilman Burns, whose experience included large art-works, believed that a wooden likeness of the Serra statue could capture the spirit of the original. He presented his concept to the members of the Channel Island Woodcarvers Association. The carvers agreed. The wooden form, Burns suggested, could then be used as a pattern for making a mold in which to cast a bronze statue, thus giving birth to the concept: "From concrete, to wood, to bronze."[13] The carvers agreed and excitement grew among them as they discussed the possibilities; 30 volunteered to help.

Early in 1986 Councilman Burns officially presented his proposal to the San Buenaventura City Council in the form of a motion. The motion "To endeavor to replace a crumbling 50-year-old concrete statue of Father Junípero Serra" carried unanimously. In the excitement Deputy Mayor James Monahan, caught in the spirit of the moment, declared the statue to be "our 'Statue of Liberty.'"[14]

On December 21, 1986, the above action prompted the following statement by the editor of the *Star Free Press*, "It was divine providence that brought Junípero Serra to the site of San Buenaventura, and divine providence is still at work because the City Council happens to include someone with artistic credentials, Russ Burns. He is an artist who specializes in large works. His enthusiastic involvement offers assurance that Father Serra will be preserved faithfully and artistically." Thus the work of preserving San Buenaventura's historical integrity was assured.

By late 1986 it had been determined that the concrete Serra statue would be replicated in wood. Burns said that carving would be done in three stages. An apprentice would "rough" the pieces, a carver would add more details, and a master carver would complete the work.[15]

FUNDING THE REPLICATION

Burns formally announced that the massive woodcarving would be used as a pattern for a bronze statue that would replace the one of crumbling concrete. In February of 1987 Burns was placed in charge of the project. Wilbur Rubottom, a professional carver and member of the Channel Island Carvers Guild, was appointed Master Carver.

Mayor John Sullard established the "Father Serra Restoration Committee." A "Father Serra Trust Fund" was set up and an old downtown building, the Old Livery, was rented by the city where the work would take place.

Fervor flourished rapidly as Deputy Mayor James Monahan addressed a letter to the Community Services Chairman requesting the Overseeing of the Father Serra Trust Fund—donation checks to be made out to "City of San Buenaventura, Father Serra Trust Fund."

In a letter to Council February 9, 1987, Monahan reiterated his descriptive phrase, "Father Serra is our 'Statue of Liberty,'" adding, "he belongs to all of us. We will work diligently to see that he remains in front of the City Hall, keeping watch over the city."

Activities now rose to an exhilarating crescendo and several distinguished figures, immersed in the extraordinary undertaking, also took up the refrain, "It's our 'Statue of Liberty.'"[16]

As plans to obtain funds developed, City Manager John Baker, in a letter to City Council on June 7, 1987, recommended that $15,000 be authorized for "start-up" of fund-raising activities of the Father Serra Statue Restoration Committee.

A fundraising committee was formed and interested people were appointed. David Eaton, former Ventura Mayor, was appointed chairman. Carol Green, City Hall Administrative Assistant, was appointed Project Manager. The committee's goal was to replace the statue by July 1988.[17]

Charles Kubilos, local artist and member of the fundraising committee, created a Serra statue miniature clay model, which was reproduced in bronze. Copies were distributed to donors of $3,000 or more.

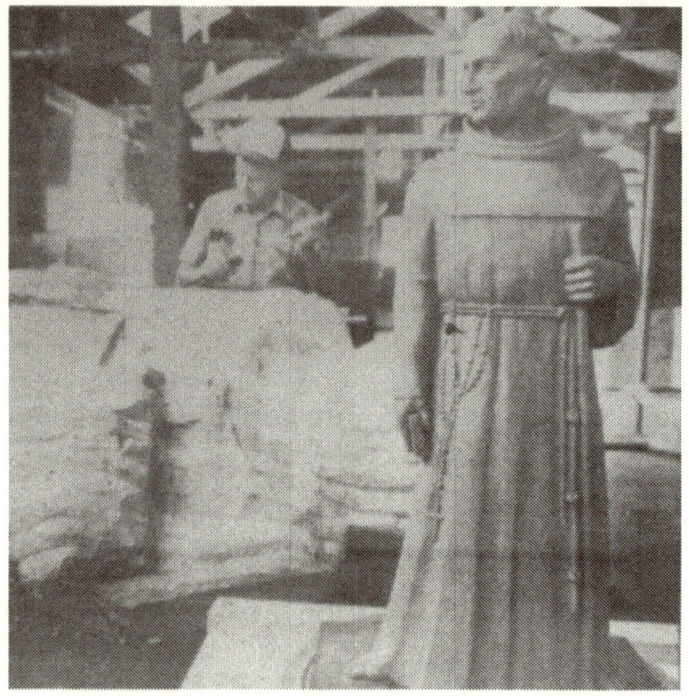

Minature Statue

Daily, between 5:00 a.m. and 9:00 a.m., the enthusiastic voices of Dave Ciniero and Bob Adams of the "Dave & Bob" show from KVEN-Radio could be heard reporting on the carving progress, praising the virtues of the project and encouraging people to respond to their spirited monetary appeal.

The *Ventura Star Free Press* also kept the story constantly alive in the public eye with vivid photos of the carving activities and numerous essays.

An energetic variety of fundraisers continuously breathed new life into the venture. Assisted by an outpouring of publicity, word spread quickly throughout the county. Enthusiasm grew by leaps and bounds. No other volunteer community project had stirred such level of interest. The carving was the talk of the land.

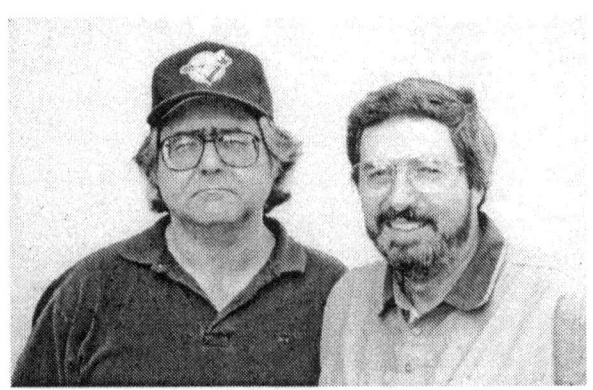

Dave Ciniero and Bob Adams, KVEN Ventura, AM radio

"Father Serra Days" were held in schools and places of business. Adults and children who gave of their dollars and pennies proudly wore their "I Support the Serra Statue" caps, tee-shirts, and pins which were sold at all community special events.

Ted Harris, 12, Student Council President at Cabrillo Junior High School, brought in $150.00; the young student had sold ice cream at a profit in school.

Ventura Jaycees "roasted" the local sheriff, netting a donation of better than $5,000, and corporate challenges were not lacking.[18]

Serving on the fundraising committee were David Eaton, Chairman; Sharon Davidson; Bob Gregorchuk; Edna Mills; Shirley Weeks; daughter of artist John Palo Kangas; and Betty June Verity.

"Bob and Dave" of KVEN-Radio persisted in their tireless appeal for funds from the public while Charles Kubilos produced bronze Serra statue miniatures. By October 20, 1988, an incredible sum of $102,119.50 had been collected with much more to come later.

In addition there were a number of in-kind donations by the American Welding Company, Leon Zermeno of OST Crane Service, and Ventura Lumber Company.[19]

Resolution
Relative to commending Dave and Bob of KVEN Radio

WHEREAS, The City of San Buenaventura from time to time, gratefully acknowledges residents who perform civic acts high in STATURE by issuing proclamations of STATUTORY significance; and

WHEREAS, Dave and Bob—or is it Bob and Dave?— have indeed performed aforementioned acts of STATUTORY significance in the service of the Father Serra Statue Restoration Fund; and

WHEREAS, during those aforesaid tender, half-awake early morning hours, Dave and Bob have also raised of Statue Consciousness in our community by the cheerfully aggressive, not to say relentless, and not-very-subliminal promotion of Father Serra Trust Fund activities; and

WHEREAS, Bob and Dave in promotion of said activities have engaged in the unshamed hawking of Father Serra tee-shirts over the radio waves, and through the U.S. Postal System they have affected the leaf-letting of all City residents with appeals for charitable cash, and during Vegas Night at the Holiday Inn and the pleasure craft convention of the Channel Dash they have cajoled would-be holiday makers and power boat racers for contributions large and small, so that all Ventura consumers of land, sea and air were daily solicited for funds; and

WHEREAS, Dave and Bob did acknowledge all contributors, large and small, on the air, so that everyone everywhere in the community would be cognizant of everyone else's largess in this great civic cause; and

WHEREAS, Dave and Bob's promotional activities have goaded the community into thousands of contributions

21

of monumental significance, so that the Father Serra Trust Fund more than achieved its fundraising goals; and

WHEREAS, Bob and Dave, did perform said service in a timely manner before our City's own "Statue" of Limitations has run out, which was about to result in a crumbling pile of concrete, but now will be transformed into a gleaming bronze beacon on the hill 9′ 4″ in stature.

NOW, THEREFORE, we, the City Council do hereby enact a STATUTE to Dave and Bob proclaiming the collective twenty hours within the week of July 11 through July 15, and between the half-awaking hours of 5:00 am to be the official

Dave and Bob Show Half-a-Working Week
Within the City limits of the City of San Buenaventura and any "receptive" airwaves beyond its environs.

Enacted on this date and time, Monday the 11th of July in the year of 1988

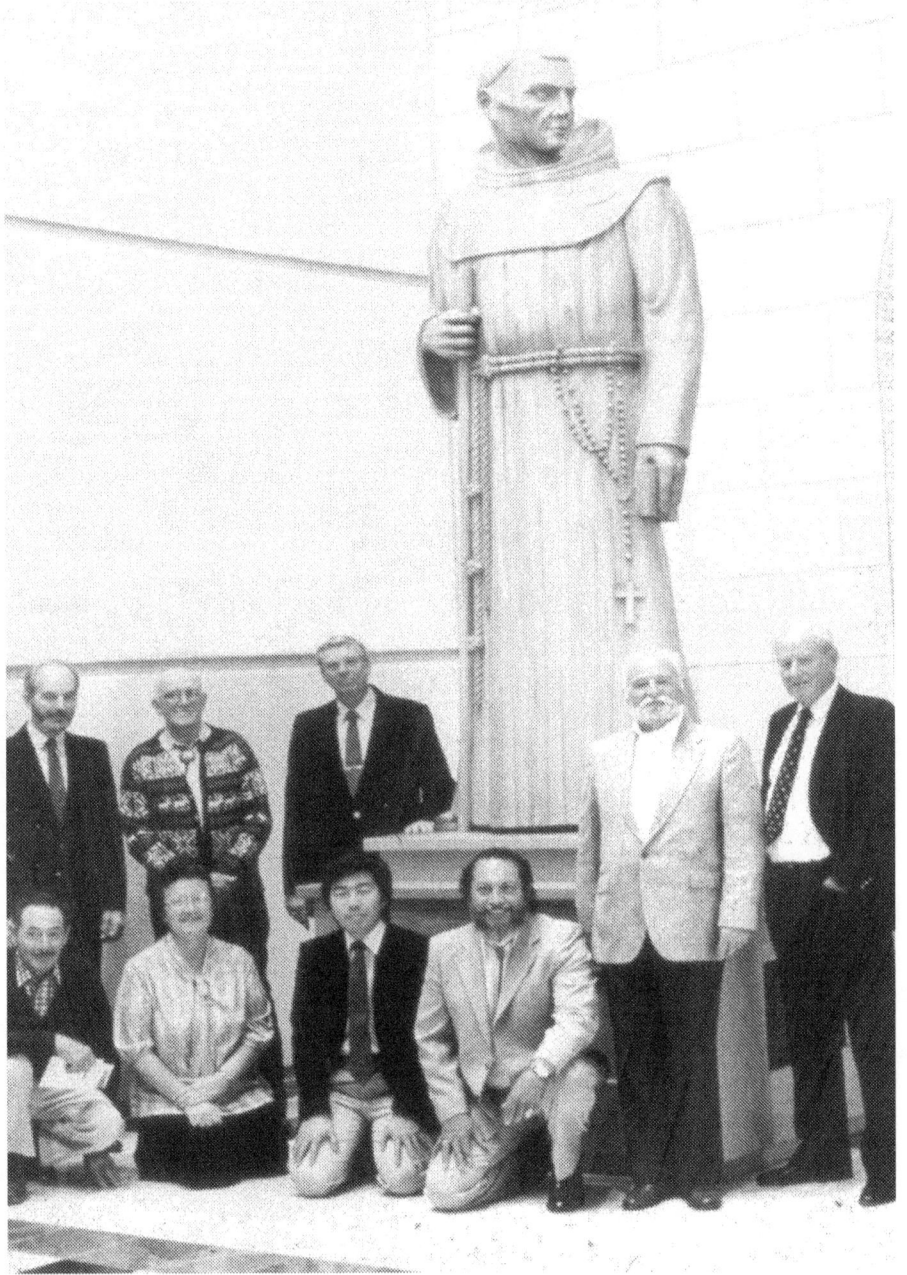

Team that carved throughout the entire project—Kneeling, L-R: Russell Burns, Judy Monzo, Bob Harada, Carlos Magallanes. Standing, L-R: Jack Holman, Joe Haugen, Sid Rundell, Richard Kamplain, Wilbur Rubottom

Catherine Antolino Mervyn
THE WOOD STATUE

As time came for the unprecedented work to begin, Russell Burns' creativity came fully into play. The concept—"to copy the original in wood," make rubber molds from it, and then cast a bronze replica, was conceived by Councilman Russell Burns in 1987.

To copy in **wood** was the unprecedented factor!

Burns initiated the remarkable task by creating a measuring device—a steel box frame in two parts, front and back (the height of the statue)—with 33 vertical and 27 horizontal slots used to measure all around the concrete statue at 3" intervals. The box was placed over the statue with a crane, and 1,782 points of reference were taken on the statue.[20]

From the measurements Burns first cut strips of plywood about 3" thick. When glued together the strips formed a reverse image or *intaglio*, popularly dubbed a "cradle," by the local newspaper. Burns, the engineer, also built a serial plane figure at that time to give the carvers a beginning. The figure, however, proved to be useless to the fine artists, the carvers.

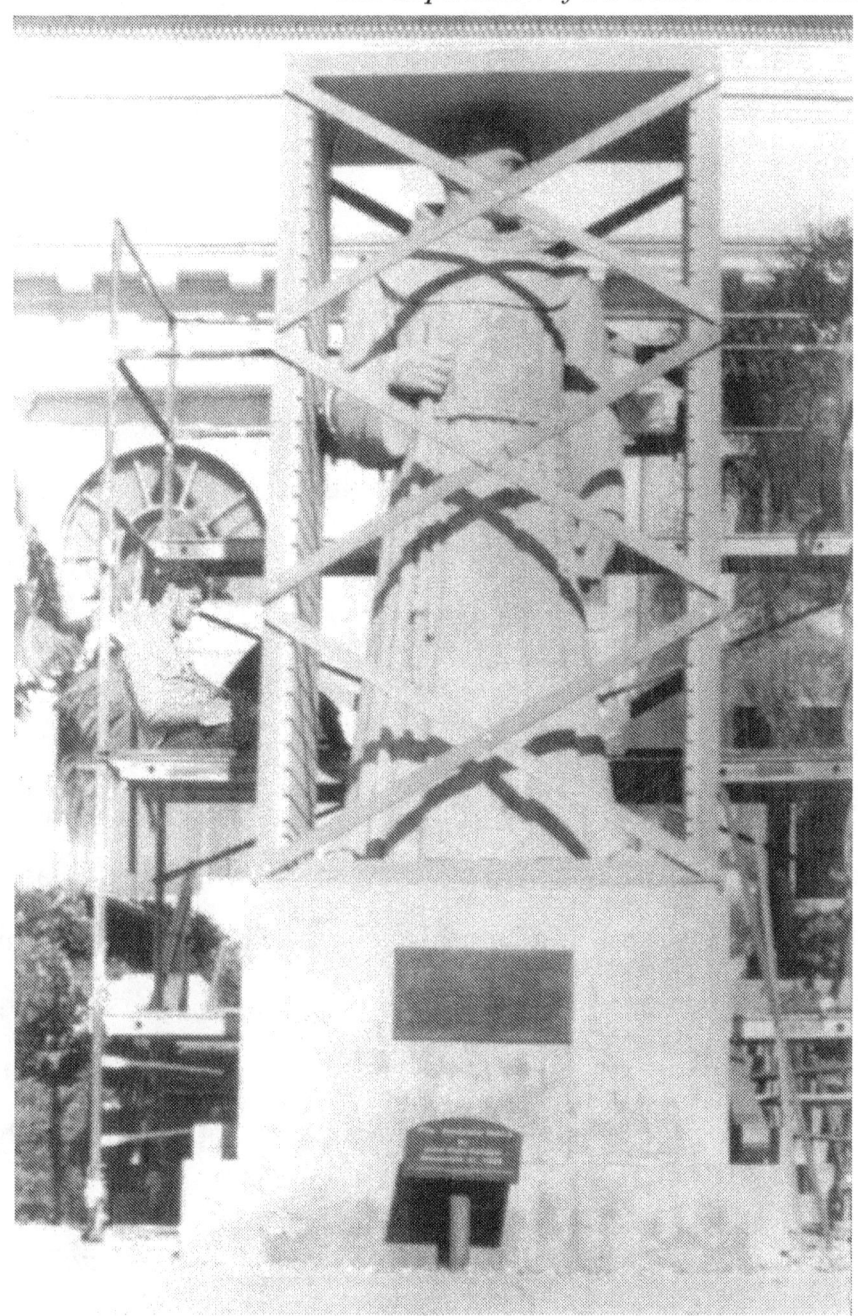

Russell Burns' steel measuring device to obtain points of reference

"An *intaglio* is a term applied to any recessed carving from which no part projects beyond the original face of the material."[21]

Webster's Unabridged Dictionary also defines the term as "a reverse mold into which other materials may be poured or pressed."

Such an instrument was used to complete the *Statue of Liberty* by Frederic Auguste Bartholdi and his craftsmen.[22]

While Bartholdi was creating an original statue, Burns was replicating an existing one—**in wood**.

The purpose of Burns' device was to measure around the statue. It took a second craftsman to complete the task.

Bartholdi first made drawings of the desired statue. From the drawings he made a full-size wood and plaster model. Over the wood and plaster model, Bartholdi built his *intalgio* or reverse image. Finally, with his craftsmen, he completed his masterpiece by pressing sheets of copper into the *intalgio* which yielded the positive copper image, the *Statue of Liberty*.

In a word, Bartholdi's wood-and-plaster model was the equivalent of Burn's concrete statue.

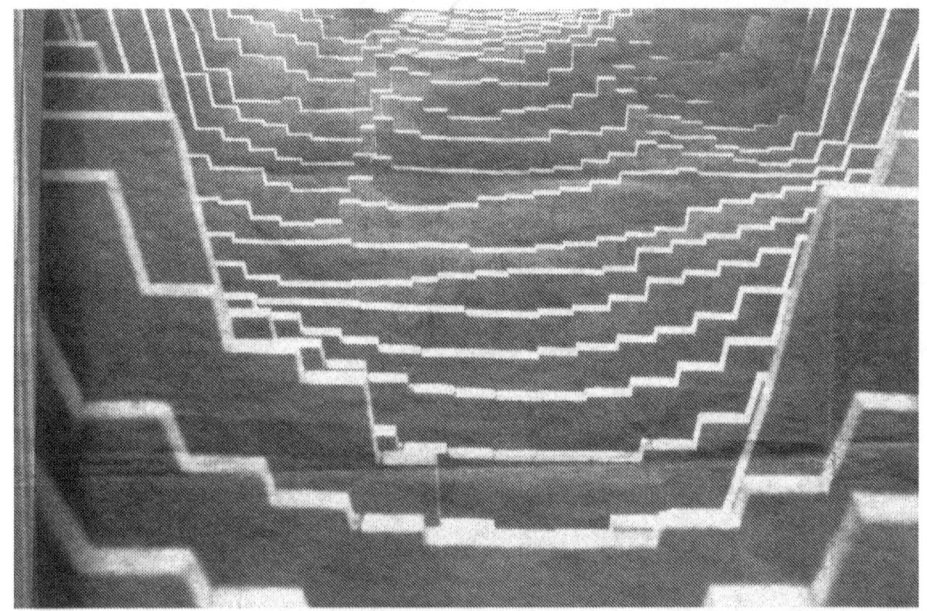

The cradle/intaglio

A recent film produced by Ken Burns (no relation to Russ) and shown on PBS TV June 27, 1992, details the construction of the *Colossus* by Bartholdi.

In a review of the film, narrated by historian David McCullough, Robert P. Lawrence writes: "Burns [Ken] has found a wealth of photos of the construction of the *Statue of Liberty* including the earliest drawings of Bartholdi, the sculptor who wanted to build a statue unlike any ever built before."[23]

Rubottom, with his craftsmen, used Burns device to obtain measurements and to take detailed photographs of the existing statue. More than 4,000 charts, drawings, grids and photographs were made from the measurements.

While Bartholdi made his drawings from his imagination, Rubottom and craftsmen made their charts, grids, and drawings from Burn's measurements of the concrete statue. They prepared for the carving process by cutting long strips of basswood to fit into the cradle or *intaglio*, thus beginning a rough outline of the statue. These strips were glued together to form a hollow block 9'5" long, 50" wide, and 33" deep. The block was first glued in two sections—front and back. The two sections were then glued together. A long iron pipe was placed through the hollow block. The block was then placed on a steel frame so that it could be turned, "like a barbecue pit," as the men joked about it later, while carving on it.[24]

On February 2, 1987, the rough form weighed nearly 1,200 pounds.[25] By mid-April 1987 carving began.

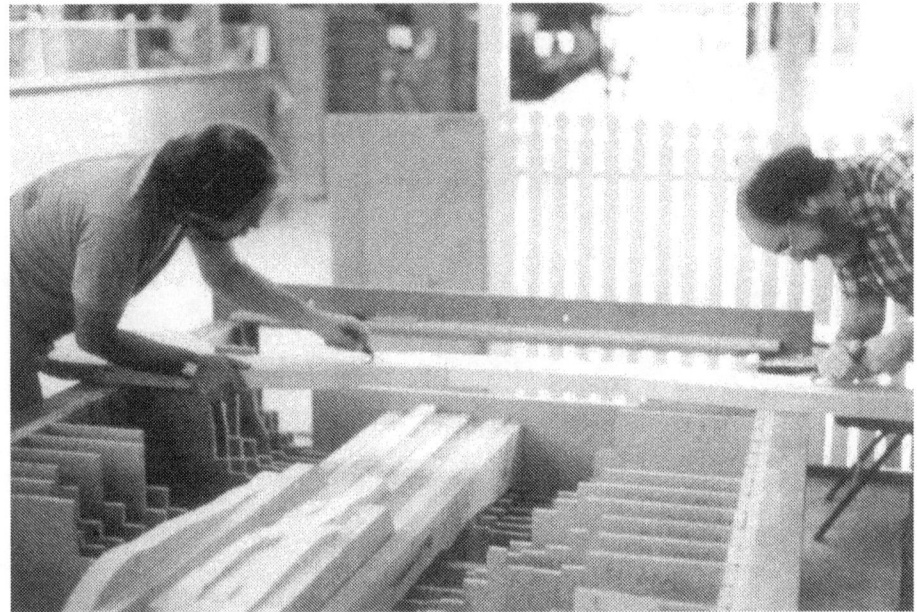

Balsa pieces cut from point-of-reference measurements taken from concrete statue

A second measuring device was made to transfer Burns' measurements taken from the concrete statue to the wood block.

The additional measuring device, designed by Burns and Rubottom, consisted of a steel frame supporting a gliding scale that could be moved along the length of the hollow block. The scale held a pencil-like vertical instrument that helped the carvers determine the depth to which

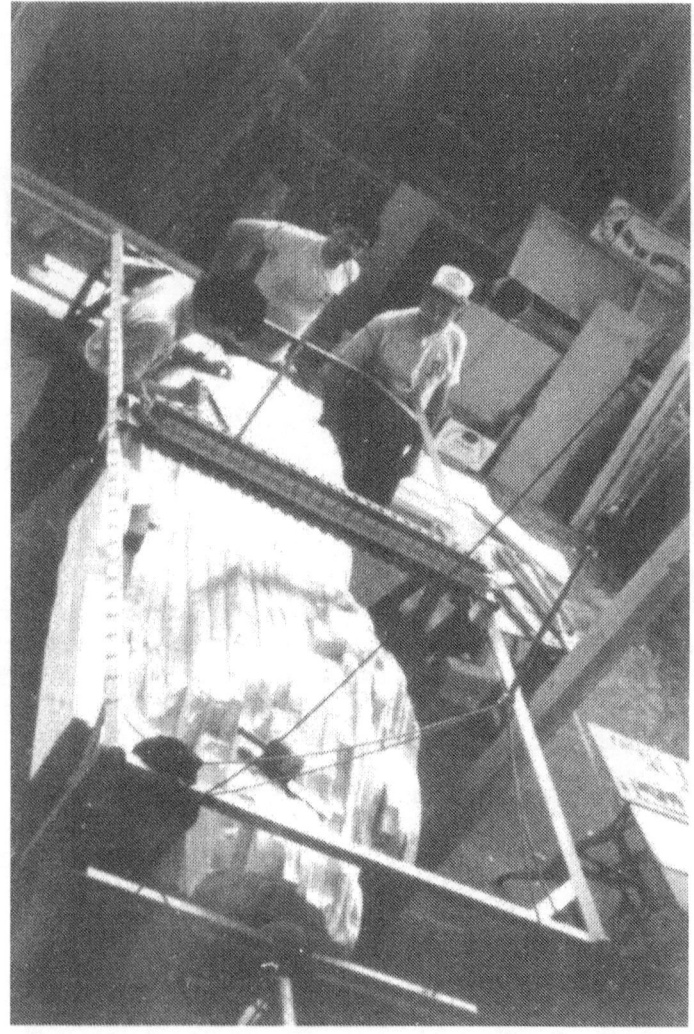

Steel measuring device designed by Burs and Rubottom made at Jim Monahan's American Welding Shop

they could carve on the hollow block in order to achieve a more precise contour of the statue. Without this additional device, carving might have exceeded the 3″ depth of the basswood strips and reached the hollow center, resulting in an open hole.

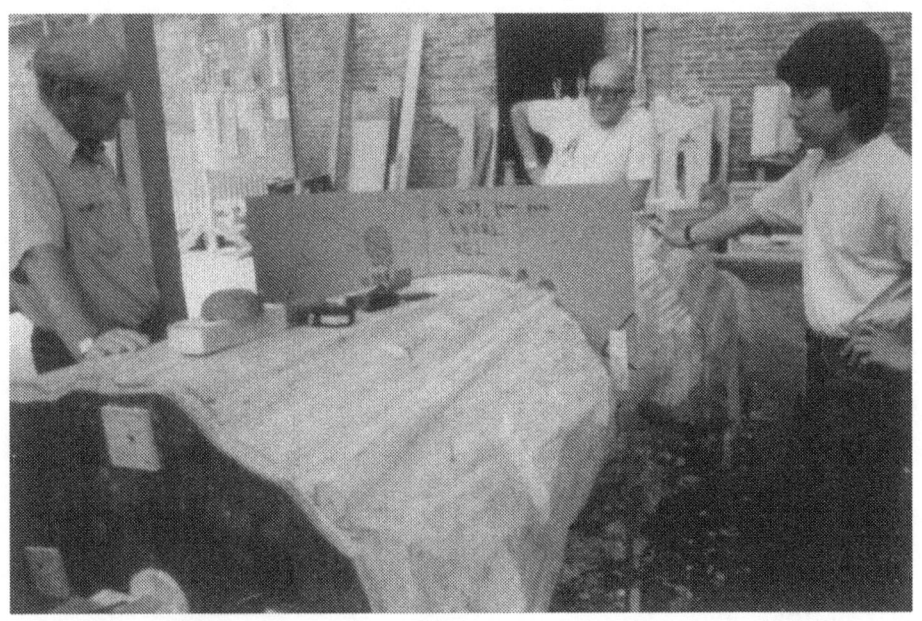

Use of templates considered crucial

Rubottom and his team of carvers, however, soon realized that the measurements they had were insufficient to proceed further with the carving; the 3" intervals of Burns' measurements were not adequately detailed to meet the requirements of the fine artistic work they would be doing. More precise, detailed measurements were needed at intervals not covered by Burns' measurements. Then, as measurements were checked and rechecked, the men

31

discovered another problem—the concrete statue was leaning backwards towards the City Hall building.

Due to excessive moisture from the irrigation of surrounding shrubbery, the concrete colossus had sunk and shifted in that direction nearly three inches. It did not stand as perpendicular as had been thought. This made a tremendous difference in their calculations.[26]

As the men discussed the situation, Jack Holman introduced a new concept: the use of templates.

Holman, a retired fireman from the Los Angeles Fire Department, had also pursued home construction, art, and sculpture; he was an expert in the art of making and using templates.[27]

Of Holman's contribution of templates, Master Carver Wilbur Rubottom said: "Holman's work in making the templates was actually an extension of Russell Burn's intaglio, but carried out to much greater detail than was possible for Burns." Rubottom considered Holman's construction and use of templates crucial to the producing of an exact likeness of the original in the final carving.

The actual carving began in April 1987.

As the delicate work got underway, Joe Haugen, a retired oil field worker, became Holman's faithful assistant. Haugen related that a large number of templates were made and used every half-inch on the 9'4" statue throughout the carving process. Daily he provided Holman with discarded cartons and plywood from a nearby furniture store for making new templates.[28]

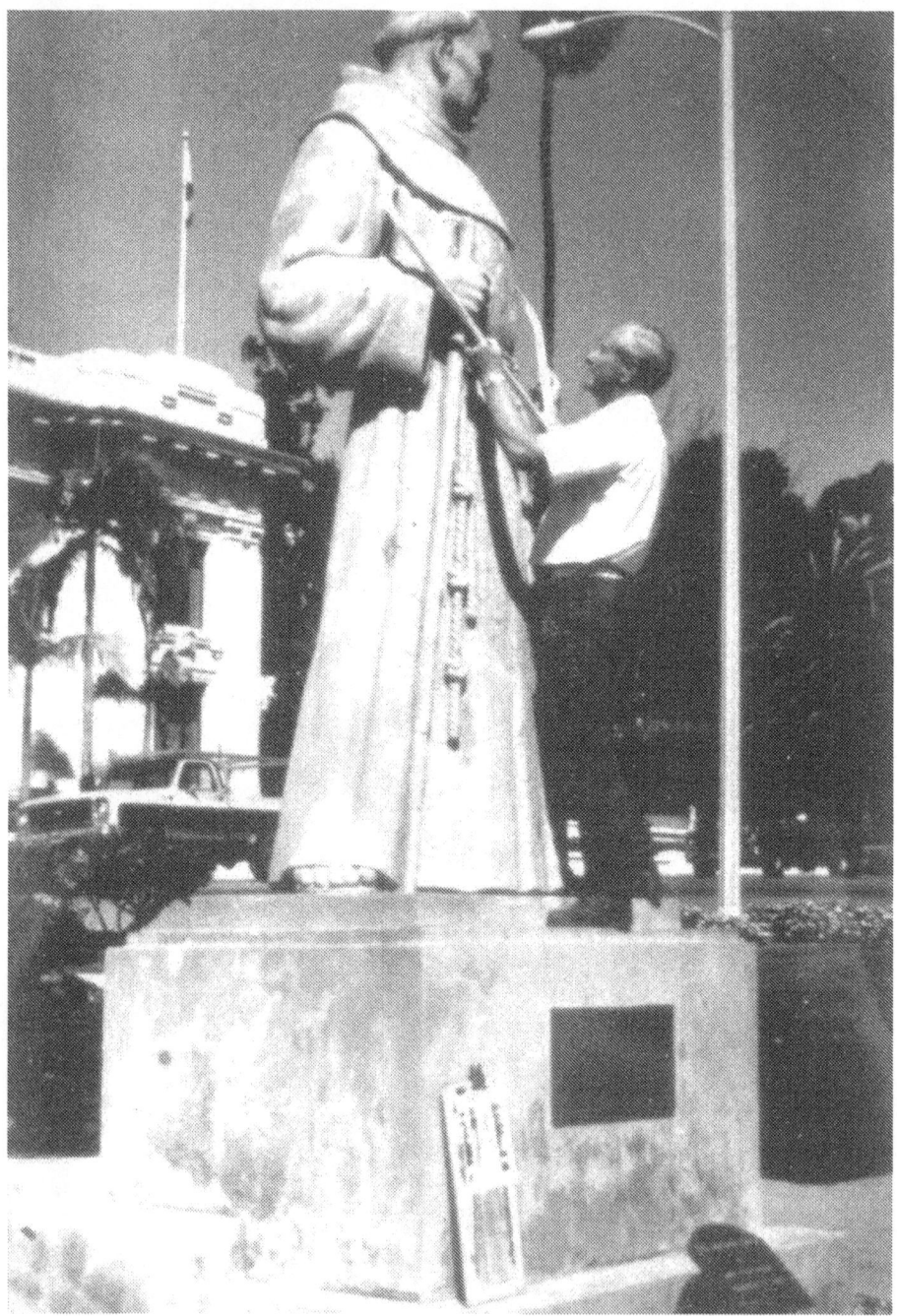

Wilbur Rubottom using outside calipers he made

While the carving was taking place under Wilbur Robottom's supervision in the Old Livery, Holman and Haugen spent many hours ascending and descending a ladder at the concrete statue site by the City Hall making and delivering templates in order to provide the carvers with the accurate measurements. The precisely made tools became indispensable and were used meticulously over the entire carving, especially around the cincture, beads, hands, feet, and any place where detailed measurements were needed.

The three levels of carving suggested earlier by Burns were not carried out. All did what they could at any time.

Master Carver Rubottom designated work almost daily to each individual volunteer based on the degree of skill he possessed in the art of carving. Guided by additional grids, sketches and a large outside caliper made by Rubottom, as well Kubelos' scale clay model, the men worked together harmoniously. Rubottom meanwhile would examine each carver's work, correct, help where needed, plan ahead, and do the more delicate finishing work. It has been said that no one would touch the head nor face of the statue; that part of the carving became entirely Rubottom's work.

In later times Rubottom's daughter, Laurie Rubottom McCoy, has related that her father, Master Carver Rubottom,

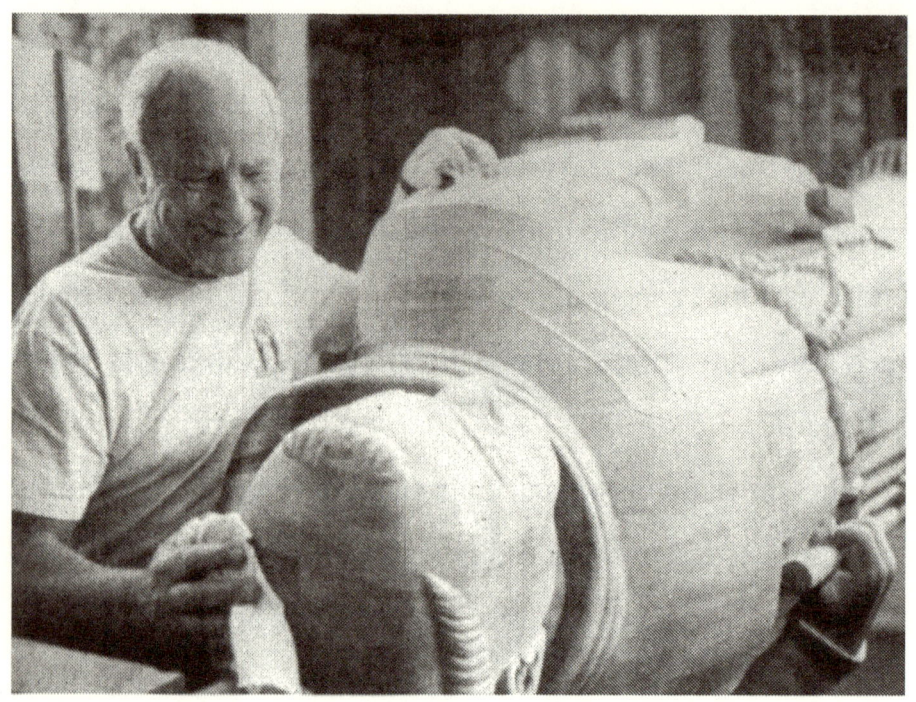

Wilbur Rubottom smiling down on face he carved

carved at least three Serra faces before being pleased with his work. (Rubottom's demise was July 10, 1993.)

Most volunteer carvers helped when it was possible for them to do so. Of the 30 men who originally volunteered, those who became regulars were Bob Harada, Joe Haugen, Jack Holman, Richard Kamplain, Carlos Magallanes (who served mainly as spokesman when visitors came), Judy

Monzo, and Sid Rundell. Rubottom alone oversaw the entire carving process.

The specialized activity became a tourist attraction. People from everywhere in the United States and foreign countries visited the Livery. Some, deeply impressed by the artistry, even wondered from where such artists had been obtained.

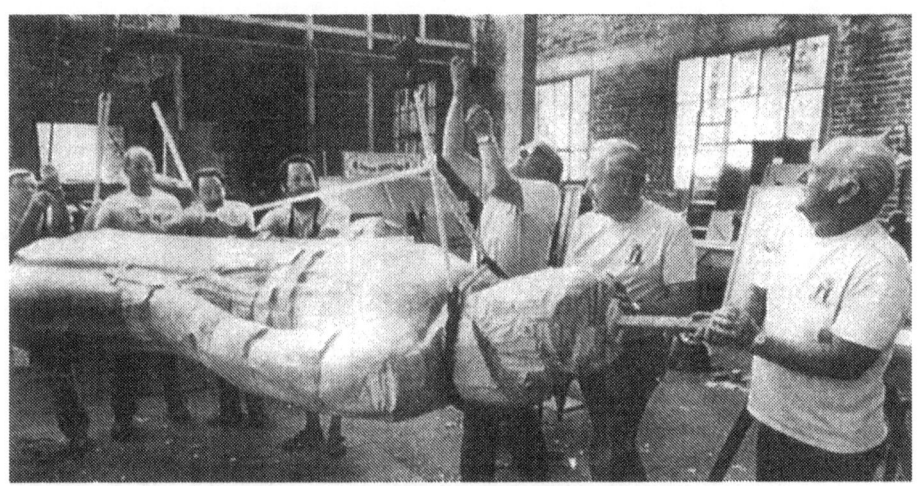

Moving unfinished statue to County Fair
where carvers continued working
Photo courtesy *The Ventura Star*

When time came for the Ventura County Fair, the gigantic wood block was transported there, where the carvers entertained visitors while practicing their craft for the duration of the fair.

All the carvers were people who were keenly interested in what they felt was a historical undertaking and cared enough to help. Each had special reasons for giving freely of his time and talent.

Some said it was a good learning experience. Others said it was a once-in-a-lifetime opportunity to do something special for posterity. All were of one accord in wanting to leave a legacy for their families by preserving a part of San Buenaventura's history. Each wanted to give "something" of himself.[29]

Among all the carvers there was one woman. Judy Monzo, a skilled carver from Camarillo, California. Her reason was even more unique, having requested to carve the rosary beads that hang from Serra's cincture.

Of Monzo, Rubottom remarked: "She did such fine work [with the beads] that people asked if the beads were glued on."

"No," they were told. The beads were carved as part of the original block.

Each day Judy traveled better than 25 miles back and forth from her home in Camarillo to the Old Livery in Ventura, to carve the rosary. When questioned why she did it, she hesitated for a moment, then finally added that she always had a "lively interest" in Father Serra. After a little urging she took a deep breath, paused for a moment, then reluctantly added: "I had a sister who was killed in an accident sometime ago; I did it in her memory."[30]

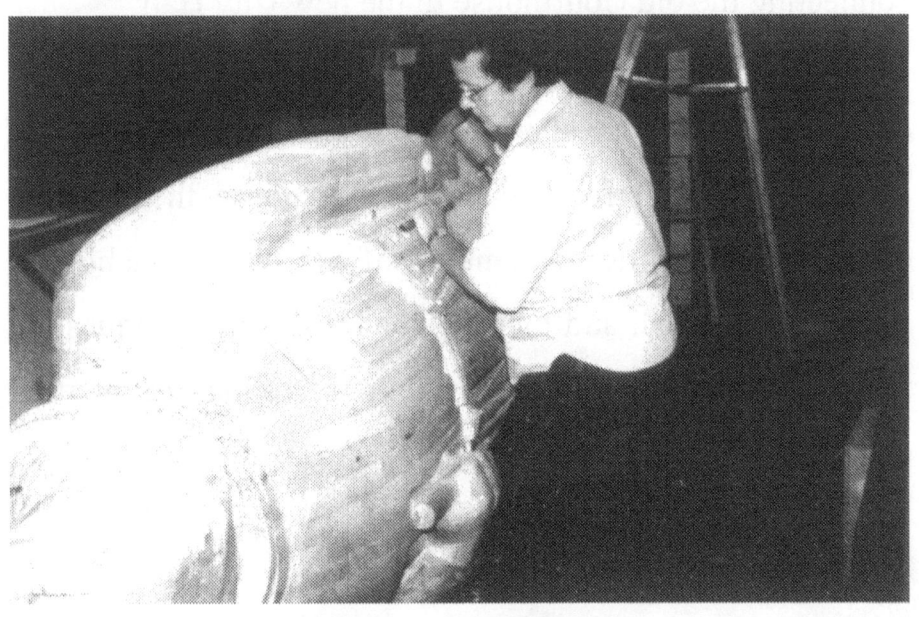

Judy Monzo carving rosary beads

The monumental carving task, begun February 2, 1987, was declared completed July 21, 1988. Master Carver Rubottom had recorded better than 10,000 donated hours of work by all carvers involved. The completed masterpiece, now weighing about 800 pounds, was ready to be used as a pattern for the casting of the bronze statue.

A question arose as to where the wood-carving might be displayed after the molds were made for the casting of the bronze statue. Three locations were suggested—the new county government center, San Buenaventura mission grounds, and the City Hall atrium—a beautiful room connecting the old Courthouse to the new City Hall.

The "Dave & Bob" show of KVEN Radio came to the rescue. A radio contest was initiated to invite listeners to decide on a preferred location. In response there was a deluge of letters from members of the newly established Padre Serra Parish and their pastor in Camarillo requesting that the statue be displayed on their grounds or in their church.

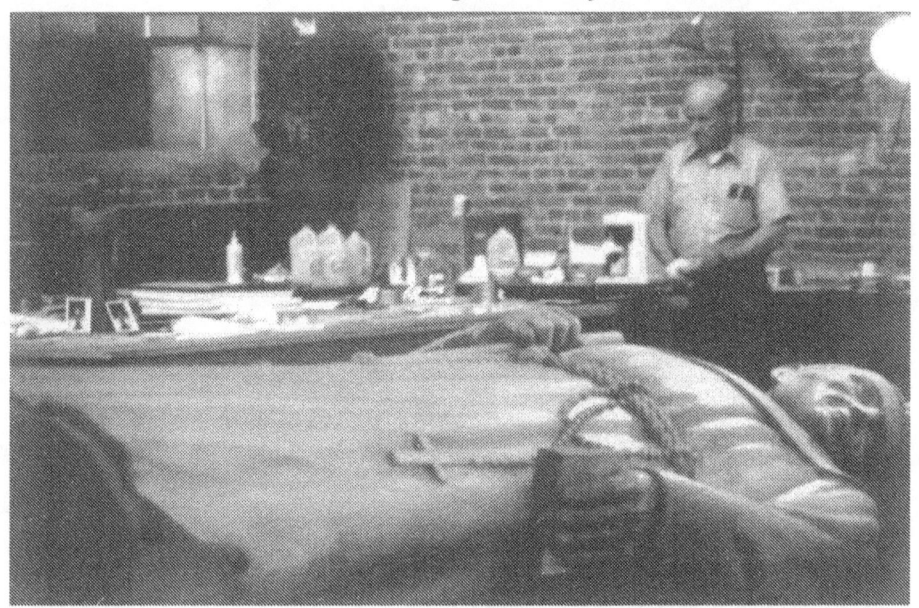

Completed wood statue and Wilbur Rubottom waiting agreement on place to display statue

An overwhelming reply, however, was in favor of the City Hall atrium as had originally been suggested by the Ventura Arts Council.[31]

A disagreement was voiced by the Candelaria Indian Council. As a group, they were opposed to the location because of some rock paintings they were planning to display there. They felt that Father Serra and the rock paintings were not compatible.

In a letter to the city's mayor, they strongly cited Serra's alleged misconduct toward the early Chumash Indians, referring to him as one who may have been a "slave driver."

An outpouring of protest arose from the people of San Buenaventura and was manifested by an enraged response from Master Carver Rubottom who placed Serra in a broader historical perspective.

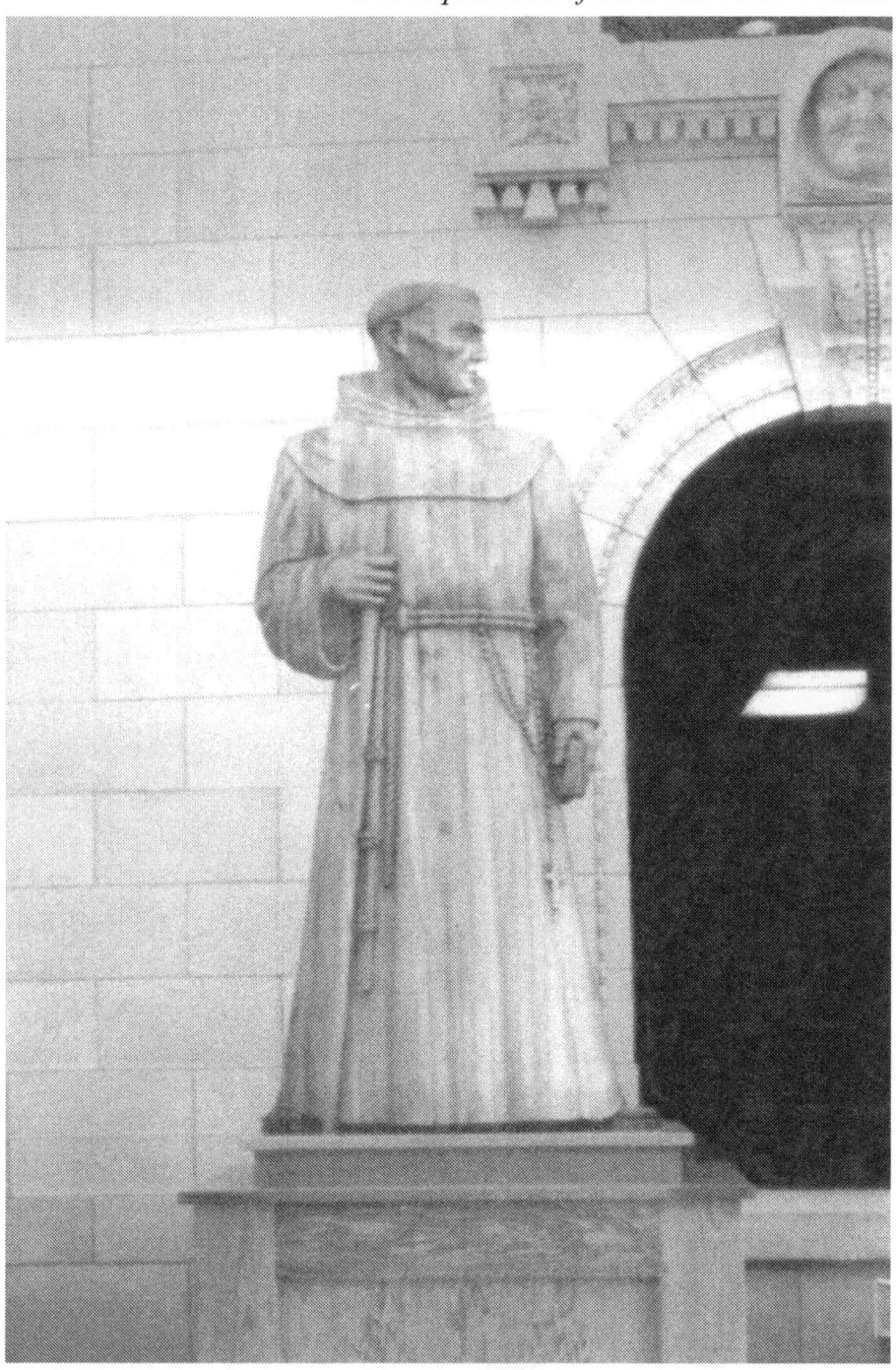

Wood statue in atrium

In a letter to the City Council, September 22, 1988, Rubottom wrote, "Father Serra's part in California's history is inextricably connected with the Chumash Indians. There is more evidence to indicate that he was their benefactor than to the contrary. If the art display in the atrium is to be an historical one, I believe the statue of Serra is just as relevant to that display as is the rock painting. Such an exhibit would be incomplete if it did not contain all of the elements present at that time in history."

Marily Kellar, Art Consultant for the San Buenaventura Arts Council in a letter of the same date, concurred, as did the *Star Free Press* in a "Vista" article (June 3, 1988).

Kellar wrote, "Father Serra [the statue] is Ventura's equivalent of Michelangelo's *David*."

The altercation was finally settled, and it was agreed that both the rock paintings and the wood statue did belong together and would both be displayed in the same location.

The wood statue remained in the Old Livery while preparations for the bronze casting were being made.

When all was in readiness, a large crane, furnished at no cost by Leon Zermino of the Oilfield Service & Trucking Company, moved the completed woodcarving to the atrium of the San Buenaventura City Hall. There the life-like form of Father Serra stands in harmony, beside the colorful Chumash rock paintings.

The elegant wood figure was dedicated on a June morning of 1988. The pleasing spacious atrium was filled with city officials and people from many parts of Southern California.

Meanwhile steps were being taken to protect the original concrete statue while removing it from in front of City Hall.[32]

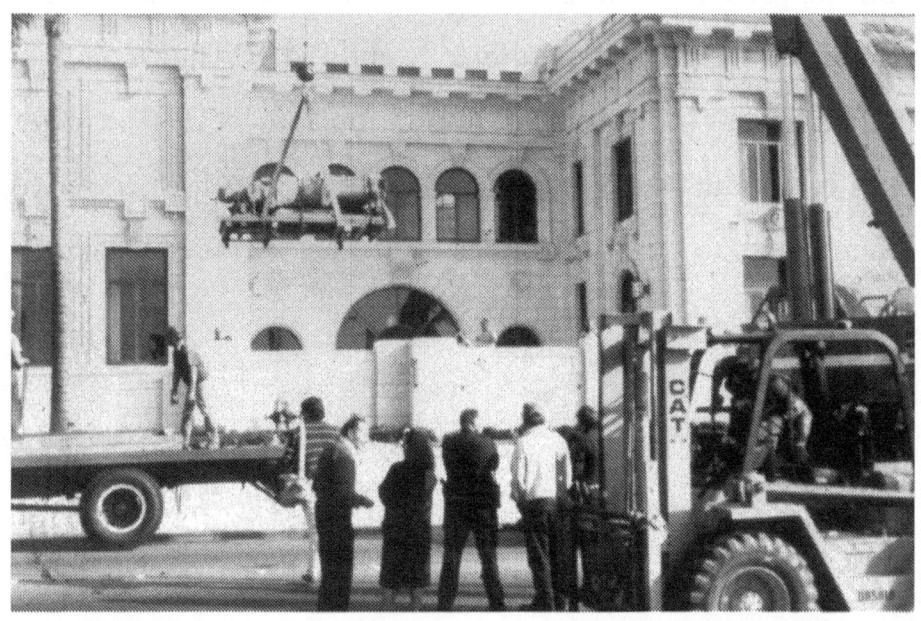

Wood statue ready to be placed into atrium by crane from American Welding

Catherine Antolino Mervyn
REMOVAL OF THE CONCRETE STATUE

The complexity of the entire enterprise was best expressed by Rubottom, who told a new reporter from the *Ventura County Coast Reporter*: "The project seems an unusual mix of science and art or mechanics and art."[33]

The truth of the statement became even more evident in the removal of the concrete statue to make way for the one of bronze.

On November 16, 1988, Russell Burns' imaginative mind approached the problem with a touch of humor. He issued a six-page "manifesto" entitled: "The Concrete Father Serra—A Statue of Limitation," in which he dealt with two main issues in the removal process: how to move it and where to put it. The need to protect it was evident.

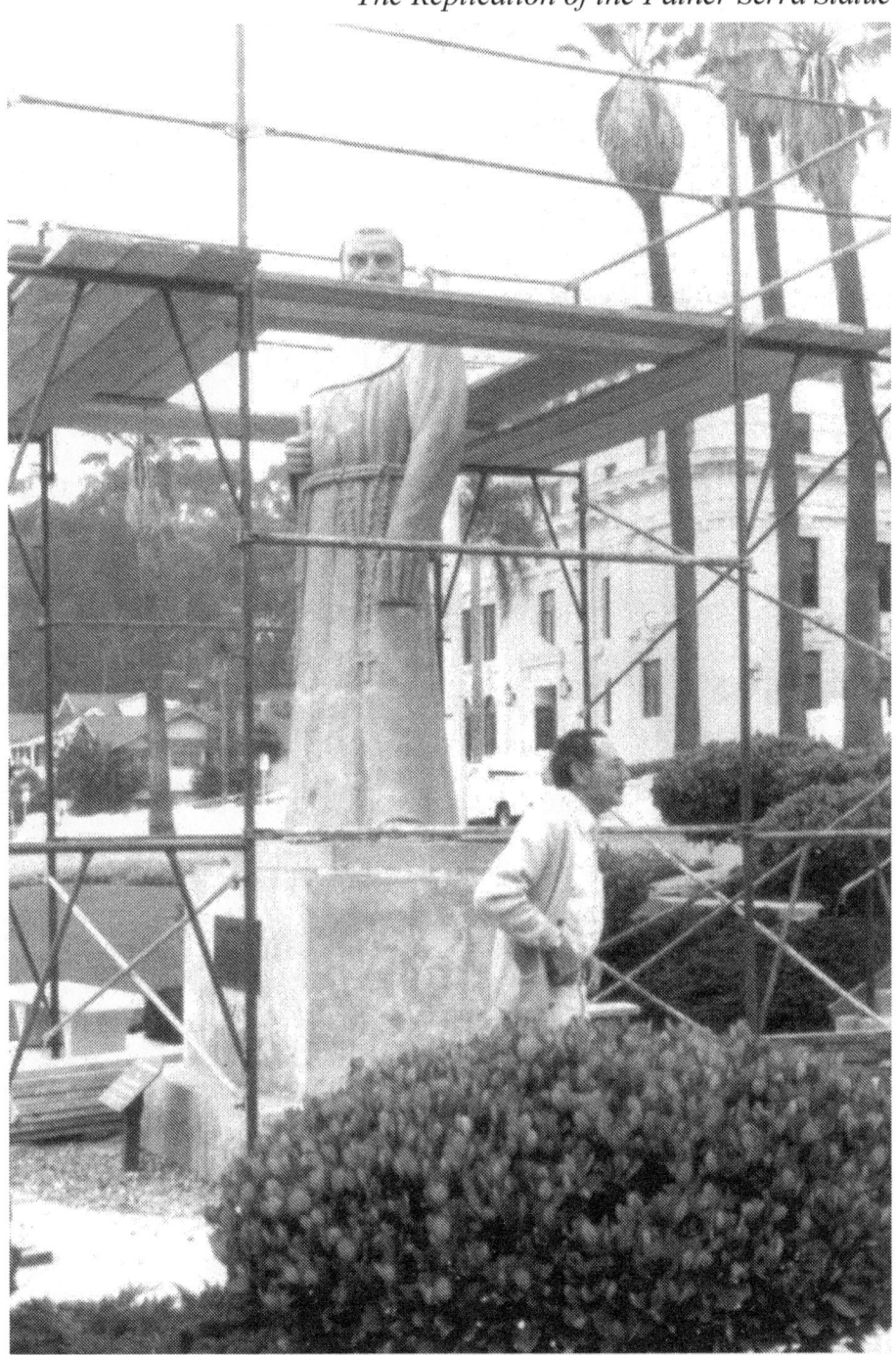

Russell Burns contemplating removal of concrete statue

In the introduction he summarized 16 specific steps which he felt were needed to be precisely followed.

Three possible locations were thoroughly examined: an inside room of the County Historical Museum, the museum grounds, the San Buenaventura mission grounds.

The interior of the County Museum was eliminated because of the difficulty of moving the statue indoors. Weight and height presented a "major engineering problem."

The museum grounds were also dismissed because of the 8' water level under the area of the museum. Burns said, "It's not worth the effort."

The mission ground was a "distinct possibility." However, any exterior location would still expose the figure to disintegration, though the process might be slowed by extensive protective measures.

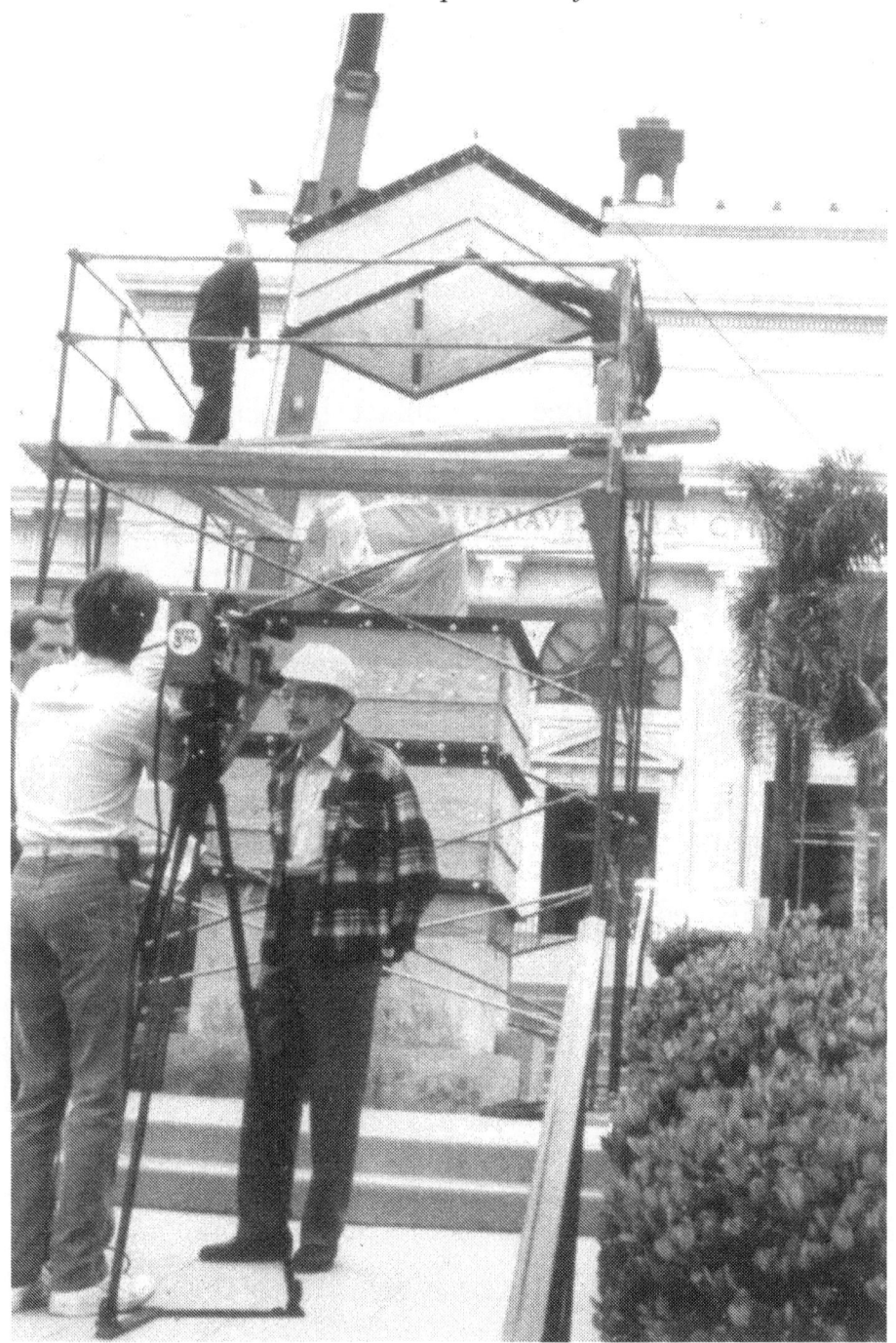

Russell Burns directing removal of concrete statue

He added: "We will need the advice of a chemist at that time, and we can't do anything to it until we have it cut from its present base."[34]

In deciding where to display the six-ton, 10' concrete statue, which needed to be kept indoors, not many options were open to the City of San Buenaventura, the owner. Finally it was decided to contact the Farm Implement Museum Committee, a branch of the Ventura County Historical Society, who planned to build a museum in Camarillo. They were pleased to accept the offer, but requested that the statue be stored temporarily until the building is constructed.

In cutting off and moving the statue, the fragility of the concrete was a problem of major concern—how to protect it and how to keep the statue from breaking—preventing the loss of the historic relic.

Burns first suggested wrapping the statue in heavy plastic—"mummy-like style," and building a box around the existing statue, which would then serve as an encasement during transportation and/or storage. Then he added, "A box will be composed of 2" x 12" horizontal boards, with 2" x 4" flange pieces all around the periphery.

Each successive box will be bolted to the preceding one, until the entire statue is encased. This modular encasement will then be filled with liquid epoxy. When the epoxy is hardened, the statue can be cut from the pedestal, laid down on its side, and the removal of crumbling material from the inside can be started."

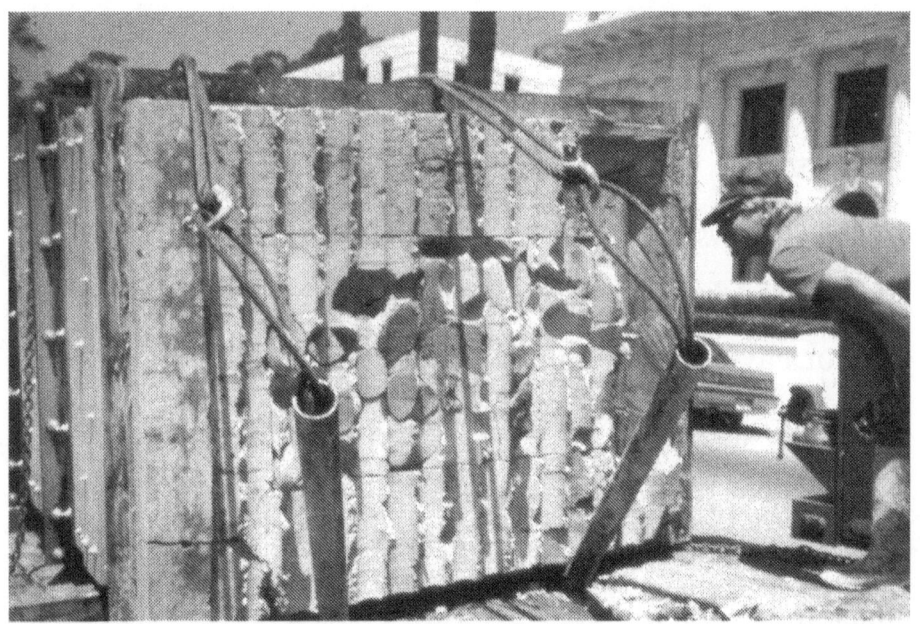

Bottom of concrete base after being sawed off from original statue

Burns then cautioned: "It would be wise not to get too ambitious about removing too much loose material from the interior because the exterior shell might cave in on us."

The epoxy mixture would also be applied to the interior of the statue.

"Once that part of the project is completed," Burns said, "the statue may then be mounted on its new base block. When completed, the outside box can be removed, one box at a time, inspecting as we go, until all of the boxes, exterior foam, and plastic wrap have been removed. We must achieve this part of the project with great caution, since we are dealing with an unknown situation, hopeful that the chemistry we wind up with will do what we want it to."

He concluded the introductory part of his document by adding: "I forgot to mention that on the final filling of the interior cavity, the statue will have to be stood on its head. No big problem—just slow and easy!"

We have no precedent that can guide us to the use of a proven method" he lamented. "There are many ways to attack the problem."

Burns estimated the total cost of removing the concrete Serra statue to be a maximum of $10,000.00.[35]

After the successful execution of most of the 16 steps outlined by Burns to protect the statue in its removal from the original location, holes were drilled in the concrete pedestal just below the feet of the historic figure, then a powerful concrete saw was utilized to actually saw the statue from its pedestal. A gigantic crane from Oilfield Service & Trucking Company lifted the encased form, loaded it onto a long truck bed, and delivered it to the same company's yard on Ventura Avenue for temporary storage.

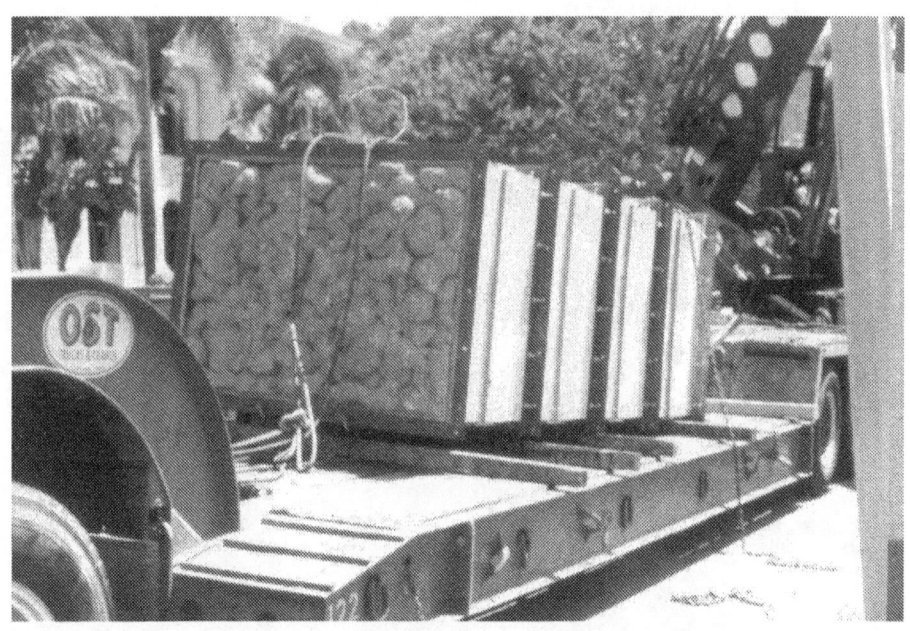

Encased concrete statue ready for storage

A close scrutiny (July 9, 1992) of the huge box—marked "Property of Ventura County Historical Museum" and lying horizontally—showed the exposed bottom of the box did not expose any "digging out of the loose soft material from the inside of the statue and refilling the cavity with some

53

form of epoxy," as stated in Burns' "Statue of Limitation" paper. Parts of eight rusted reinforcing rods protruded, probably having been placed there when the concrete was poured into the original breakaway mold.

The entire statue remained encased horizontally in the attached units which appear to be one huge steel reinforced box, filled with epoxy.[36]

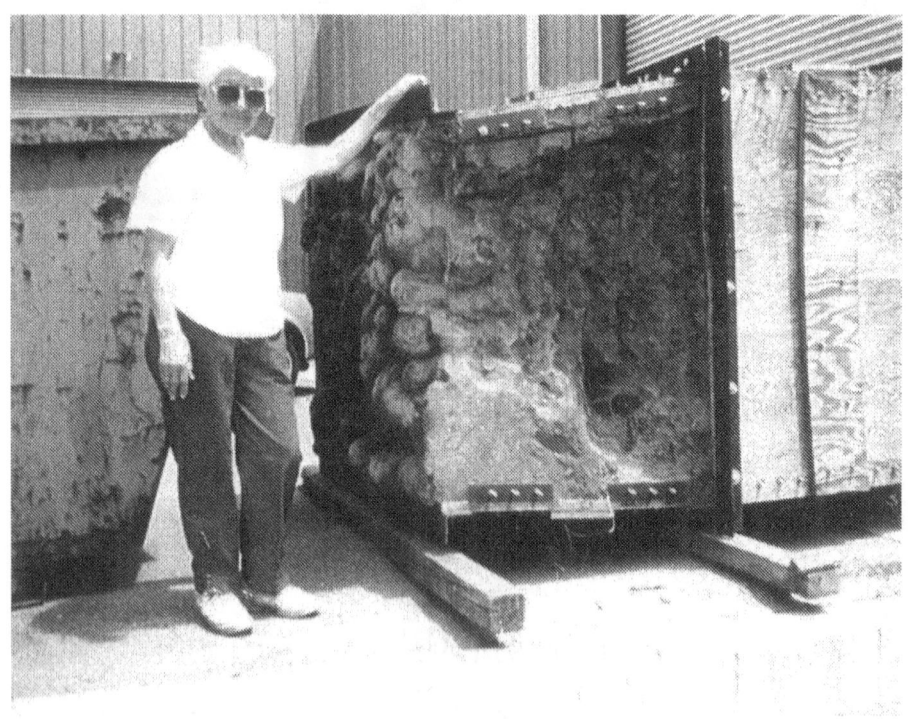

Author Mrs. Mervyn
Top end of encased concrete statue showing epoxy

Robert Pfeiler, Director of the Farm Implement Museum, who has collected a large number of agricultural implements, said that future plans for a County Agricultural Museum in the City of Camarillo included an atrium. The concrete statue is to be placed there, in the new atrium, where it will be protected from the weather and enjoyed by future generations.[37]

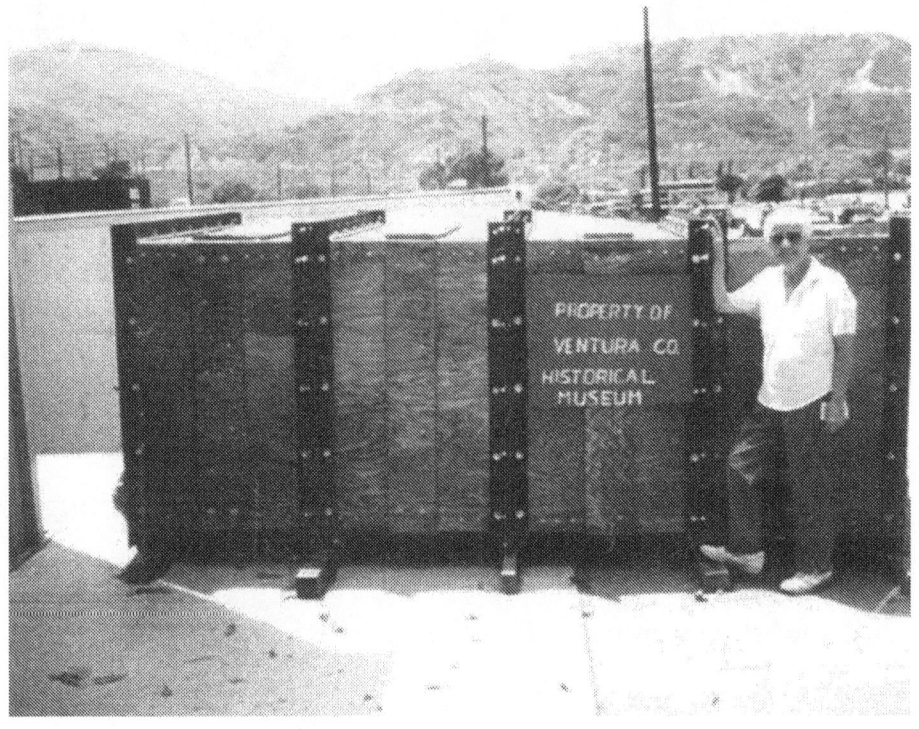

Author Mrs. Mervyn
Encased concrete statue in storage area on Oilfield Service Trucking Co. grounds, Ventura, CA

Catherine Antolino Mervyn

THE BRONZE STATUE

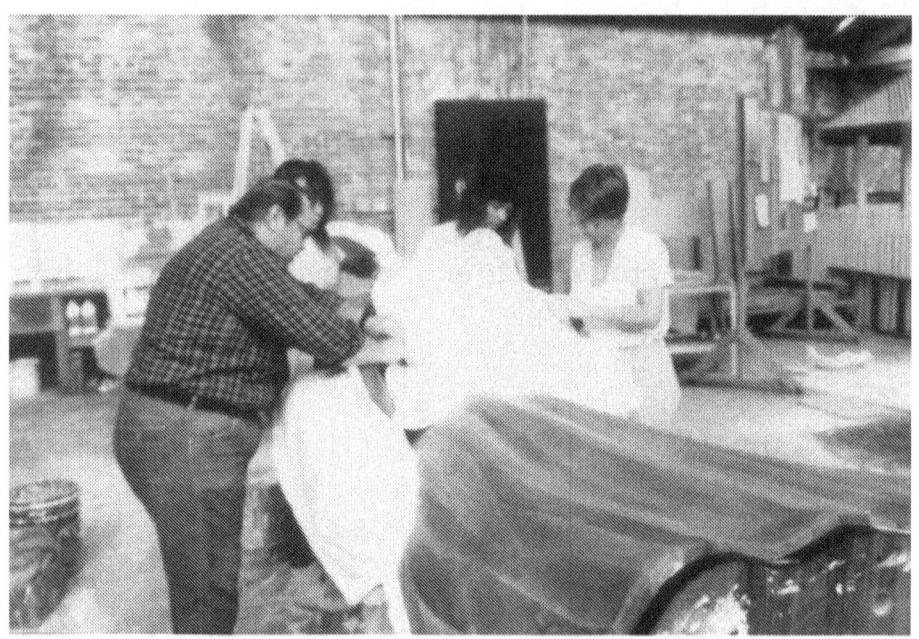

Wood statue partially covered with latex

In June 1988, before the carved wooden statue was moved from the Old Livery to the atrium in the City Hall, it was ready to do its duty as a pattern for the bronze casting.

Several bids had been submitted for the unique craftsmanship required. The California Sculpture Center at the College of the Desert in Palm Desert, California was engaged as the lowest bidder, with an estimate of $17,000 and a cap of $24,500. Professor William A. Kohl of the college faculty, in a letter to Carol Green, expressed his pleasure and honor by noting: "The uniqueness of this commission will be of lasting value to our apprentices."[38]

A team of student-craftsmen came from the college to the Old Livery in Ventura to make molds from the wooden statue. Burns' notes reflect that the statue was sectioned in 22 parts.

When Rubottom saw the unsightly rubber mixture spread over the exquisite finished carving, he was secretly horrified and wondered if it would all come off. It did—to his delight![39]

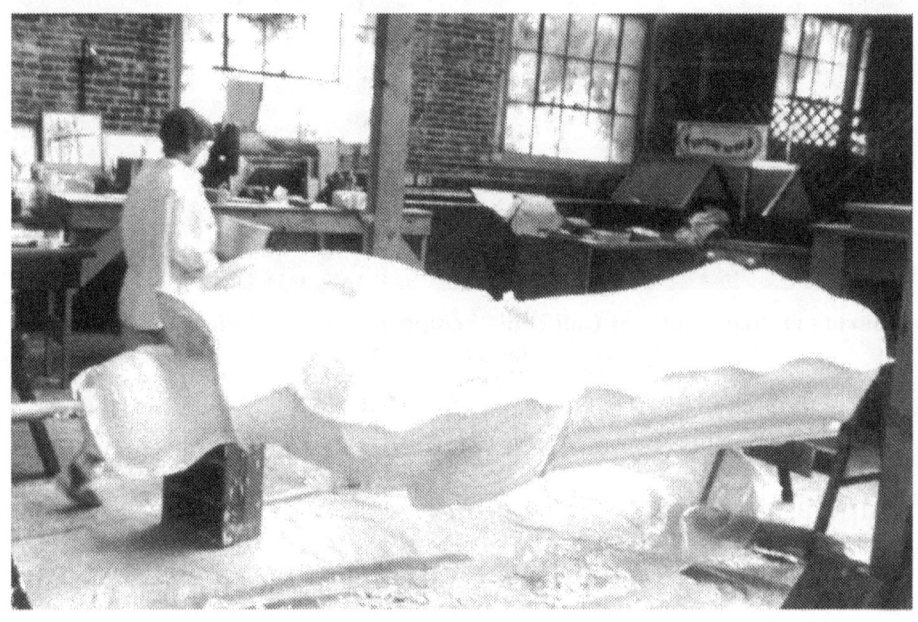

Entire Statue covered with latex

The molds made from the wood statue were delivered to the foundry for the bronze casting to be accomplished by the ancient "lost-wax" method. That is, the molds were covered with a layer of special wax, then dipped in a ceramic solution which dried to form a shell.

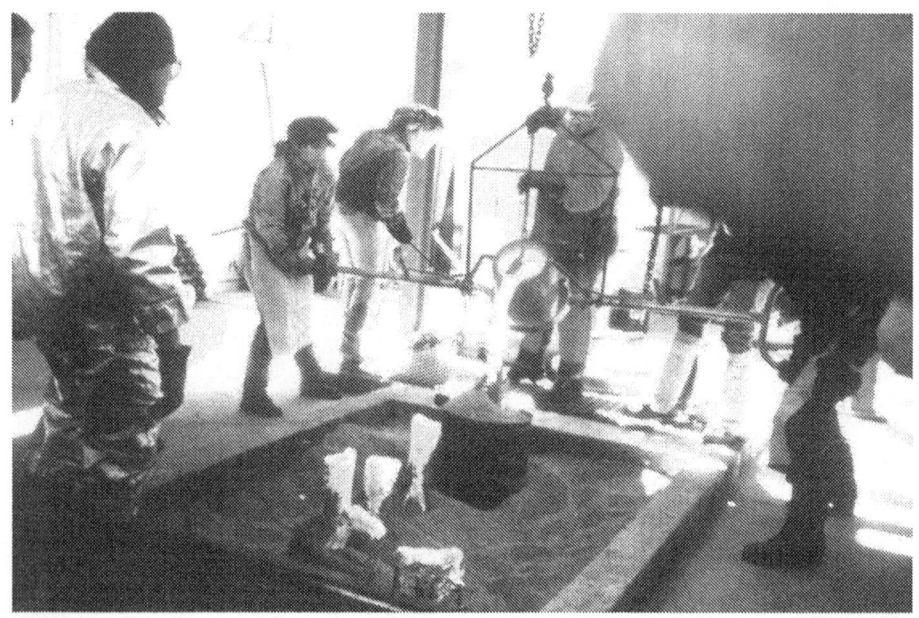

Pouring molten bronze at California Sculpture Center, College of the Desert, Palm Desert, CA

The molds were then heated in a kiln to a high temperature, firing the ceramic shell and melting out the wax. The molten bronze, a mixture of copper and tin, was poured into the molds and allowed to cool.

The result was 22 pieces of bronze, which together would compose the statue. These pieces were welded together, ground off and polished. Finally, the surface was heated to expedite oxidization, forming a protective coating known as a patina. If heat had not been applied, the protective coating would have formed naturally over a long period of time by weathering.[40]

Rubottom visited the college foundry several times as did Burns, Carol Green, Shirley Weeks, and others, while the work was in progress. On at least one occasion Rubottom was able to call attention to some important elements that needed special refinement in the casting process—some that might easily have been overlooked by the young student-craftsmen.

In San Buenaventura the City Council had authorized the sum of $2,500 from community Improvement Funds to build a concrete pedestal overlaid with black granite from the Andes Mountains in South America.

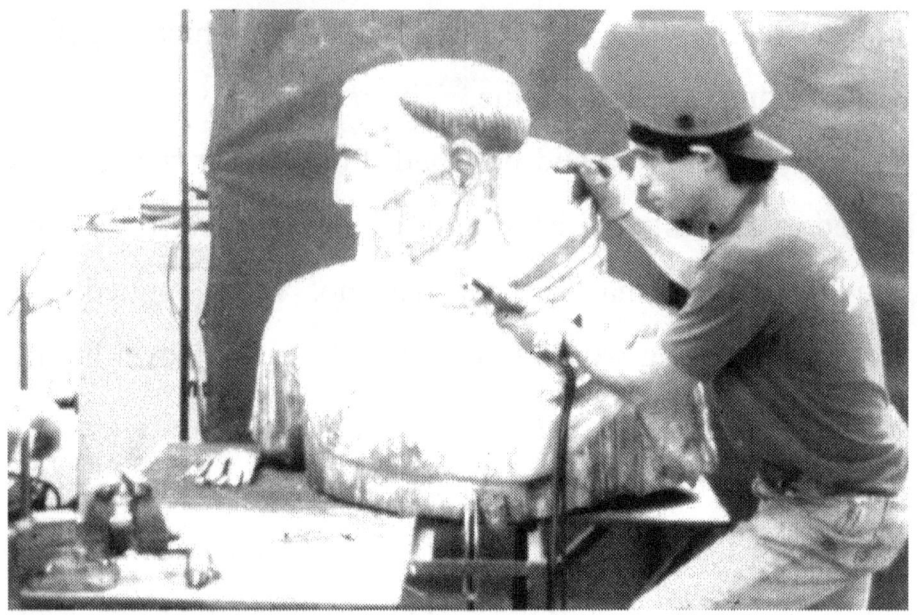

Polishing the bronze bust

Jim Taylor and Ed Pogue, associate directors at the California Sculpture Center, in a letter of August 3, 1989, mailed detailed installation instructions to Project Manager Carol Green.

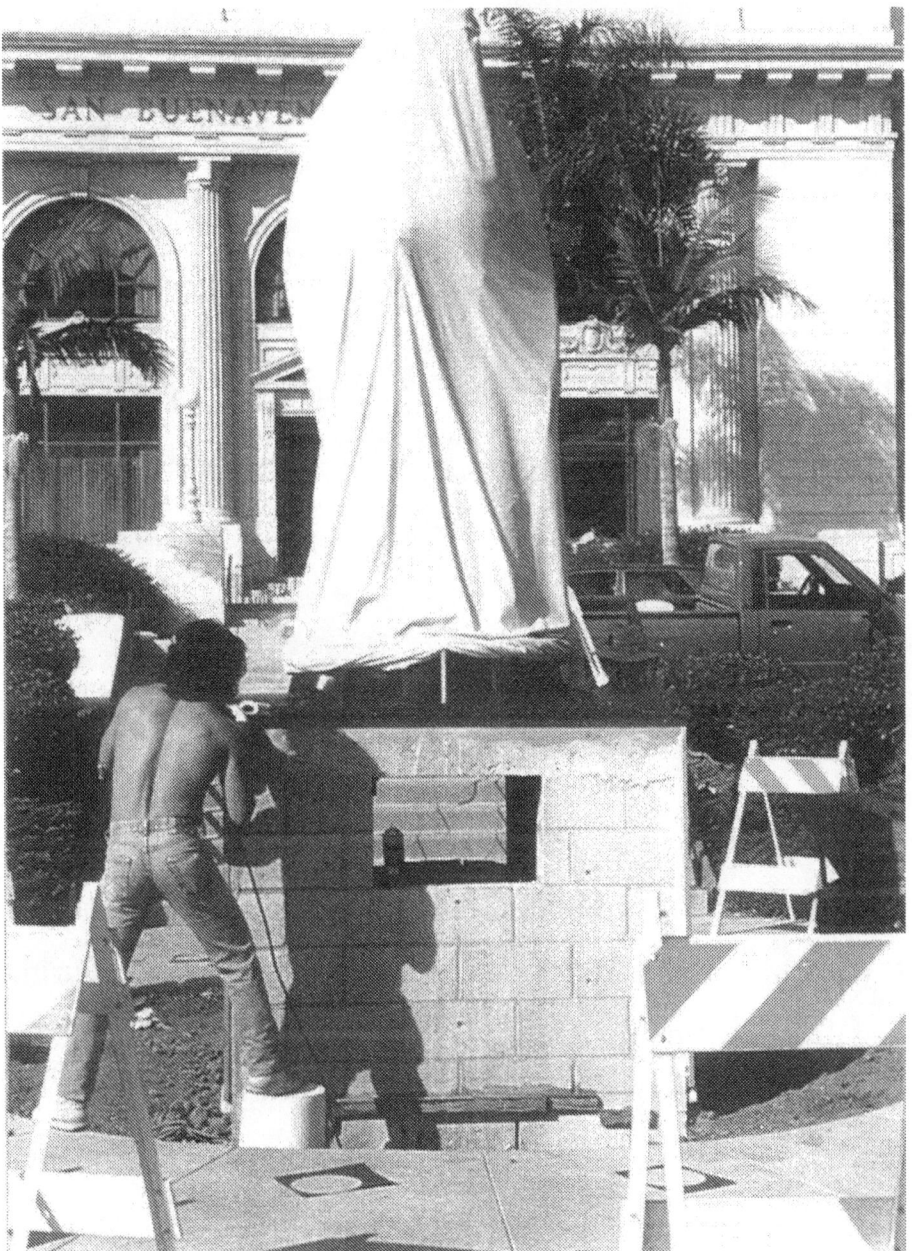

Scott McClurry of Cosa Marble Co. preparing pedestal to receive time capsule
Photo courtesy Jeff Argend

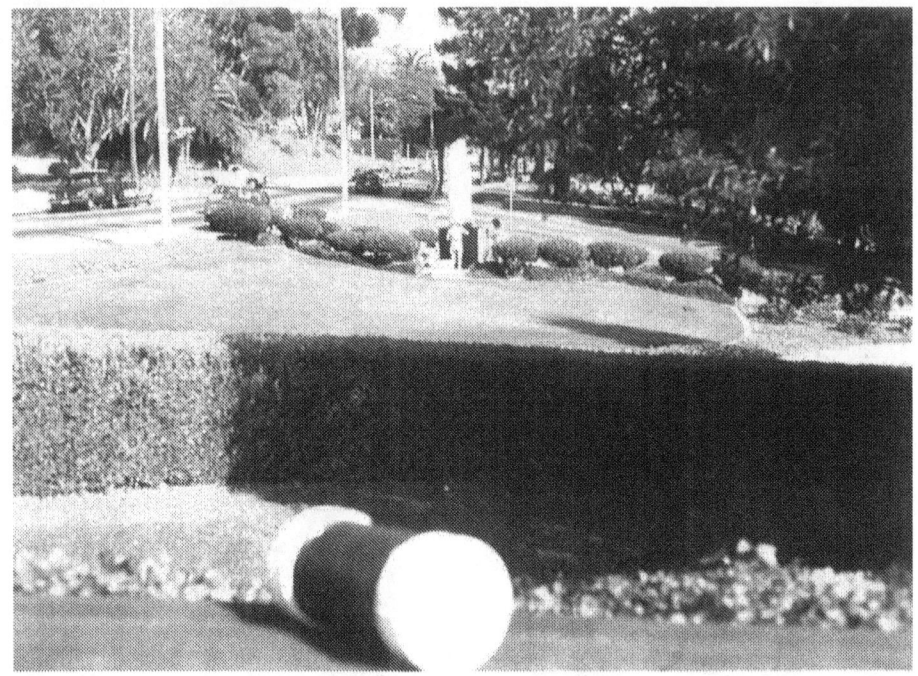

The time capsule awaiting placement
Photo courtesy Jeff Argend

Included were suggestions by Center Director William Kohl for placing a screen around the work site so that the statue might be "properly hidden from view during installations, final touch-up (patination), and detail work."

The completed bronze statue was transported back to San Buenaventura by a city truck, and was placed on the new pedestal by qualified riggers under the supervision of Russell Burns, Wilbur Rubottom, and Jim Taylor. Before the final opening in the base was sealed, Rubottom placed within the cavity, under the statue, a time capsule he and

Carol Green had put together. The capsule contained photos, news articles, office records from Carol Green, a dollar bill, and some change.[41]

Installation was accomplished in five days. The location is the exact spot where the original concrete statue had stood for 51 years.

The evening of October 20, 1989, was chosen for the unveiling and dedication of the bronze statue.

Music preceded the ceremonies and a color guard was led by the Boy and Girl Scouts of America.

San Buenaventura's mayor, James Monahan, welcomed the 500 guests who came to honor not only Serra, the "Apostle of California," but also their own remarkable accomplishments.

In his remarks Mayor Monahan added: "the statue represents our community's obsession and dedication to preserve our heritage."

Among the many dignitaries present were also the clergy from Mission San Buenaventura and Franciscan Father Noel Francis Moholy, a more recent biographer and vice-postulator for the cause of canonization of Father Serra.[42]

From California's early beginnings the people of San Buenaventura have consistently shown a special love and admiration for their city's founding Franciscan missionary, Father Junípero Serra.

Today, better than two centuries after the establishment of California's ninth mission, for which the city is named, three similar statues of Father Serra, one of concrete, one of wood, and one of bronze, stand witness to a people's dedication and passion for their historical past and faith in their future.

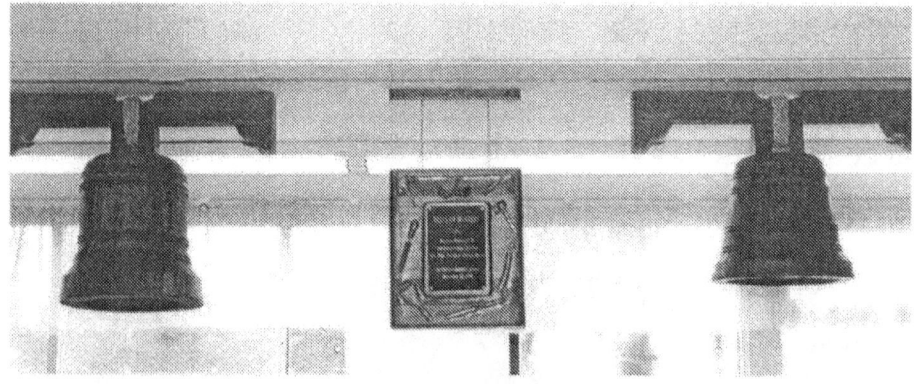

Wooden bells as replicated by the Channel Island Carvers. Photo courtesy of The Channel Island Carvers

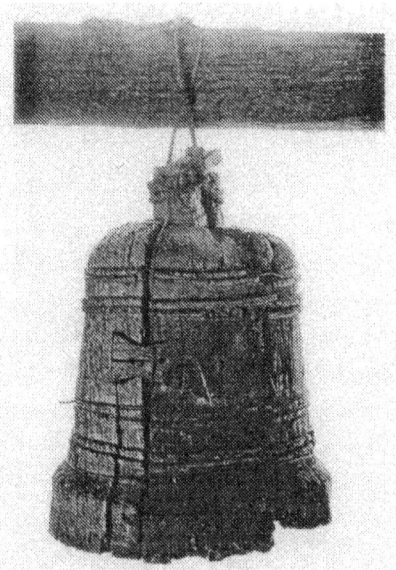

Ancient wooden bell used at the San Buenaventura Mission
Photo courtesy of the Mission Museum

Catherine Antolino Mervyn

THE WOODEN BELLS OF

SAN BUENAVENTURA MISSION

The lure of the historic California missions is remarkable. The very word "missions" evokes unparalled, tantalizing interest. Like an irresistible magnet they draw the old and the young, the serious student and the curious. Their magical appeal is universal. They are admired and derided, but always explored and scrutinized.

A recent study of mission bells by Max Kurillo and Erline Tuttle revived interest in two of the three remaining wooden mission bells believed to have been used only at Mission San Buenaventura. They are displayed among the many artifacts at the mission museum.

The bells, decayed and riddled with termite holes, have been replicated by members of the Channel Island Carvers Guild and are now on display in the new educational building in back of the mission. They were placed there to protect them from the weather. Since the demise of Wilbur Rubottom, July 10, 1993, the unique project has been under the supervision of master carver and sculptor, Charles Kubilos.

The bells differ in size. The larger is 23" in height and 19" in diameter. The replicas are composed of five slabs of mahogany donated by the Knights of Columbus, San Buenaventura Council #2498.

The original bells were cut from a large mahogany log. Each bell was made in two halves and joined by a butterfly joint. Since large logs are presently not available, each half of the new bells is carved from a block of five layers of mahogany, each 2" thick.

Leather straps that encircle the original relics and redwood pegs which apparently fasten the straps to the wooden bells, are believed by the carvers to be parts of repairs done to the bells over the years, rather than original components.[43]

The carving of the replicas took place in the wood shop classroom of Balboa Middle School in the city of San Buenaventura where the carvers still meet Tuesday evenings of each week.

Once again the members of the Channel Island Carvers gave freely of their time and talents in replicating another California historic work with the same love, devotion and professional expertise employed in the replication of the Father Serra Statue.

****

BIBLIOGRAPHY

Burns, Russell, Ventura City Councilman, Project Chairman, Phone interview, and notes mailed to author (Available at Ventura County Historical Society)

City of San Buenaventura Statue Dedication Program, Brochure, "From Concrete to Bronze," October 20, 1989 San Buenaventura City Hall, 501 Poli Street, Ventura, CA

De Nevi, Don, & Noel F. Moholy, *Junípero Serra,* Chapter. 12, p.91 Harper & Row Publisher, San Francisco, CA 1985

Green, Carol, Assistant to City Manager, Project Manager, "Serra Renovation Project Files" San Buenaventura City Hall, 501 Poli Street, Ventura, CA

Hartman, Gertrude, *America, Land of Freedom,* pp.562-567 California State Series, Department of Education Copyright, D.C. Heath & Co. 1946-1955 California State Printing Office, Sacramento 109 M-1961

Catherine Antolino Mervyn

Holman, Jack, Interview, Sept. 4, 1992

Haugen, Joe, Interview, Sept. 8, 1992

Lawrence, P. Robert, "Statue of Liberty"
Press Courier, June 28, p.27, 1992

Mervyn, Catherine—Personal visit to Oilfield Service &
    Trucking Co. grounds 2951 N. Ventura Ave., Ventura,
    CA, July 13, 1992

Minutes of the San Buenaventura City Council, 1986-1989
Serra Statue Renovation Project Files
San Buenaventura City Hall, 501 Poli Street, Ventura, CA

Monzo, Judy, Carver of Rosary
Phone Interview
Camarillo, CA

Oxnard Press Courier, Sept. 30, 1988, p.4

Pfeiler, Robert, Interview, July 23, 1992

BIBLIOGRAPHY, Cont.

Rubottom, Wilbur, Master Carver

Phone interview & personal interview

Notes available at Ventura County Historical Society

"San Buenaventura City Hall Information Agency Brochure," 1989-1990

Ventura County Coast Reporter, August 6, 1987, p.20

Ventura Star Free Press, Vista section, June 3, 1988 p.6

Ventura Star Free Press, 1986-1989, Numerous articles and photos.

Weeks, Shirley, "Comparison of Three Statues"

Two papers written for Art Appreciation—01, Ventura College

Oct. 9 & 18, 1990 (Available at Ventura Co. Historical Society)

Catherine Antolino Mervyn

NOTES

1 Hartman, G. America p.562-567

2 Weeks, S., "Comparison of Three Statues," Ventura College Paper, Oct. 1990 (at Ventura Co. Museum)

3 Ibid.

4 Ibid.

5 Ibid.

6 Green, Carol, City Hall Files, Serra Statue Renovation 1986-1989

7 Ibid.

8 Ibid.

9 Ibid.

10 Ventura City Council minutes, Burns report, early 1983

11 Ibid.

12 Ibid.

13 San Buenventura city brochure—1990

14 Minutes, Ventura City Council—1986

15 Ibid.

16 Ventura City Council minutes—1987

17 Ventura City Council minutes—1987

18 Ventura City Council minutes—1988

19 Ventura City Council minutes—1988

20 Russell Burns, Interview, August 30, 1992

21 Encyclopedia Britannica—v.12, p.456 U. of Chicago, 1947

22 Lawrence, R.P. *Oxnard Press Courier*, June 28, 1992- p.27

23 Ibid.

24 Rubottom, Wilbur—Interview, August 30, 1992

25 Rubottom, Wilbur—Interview, August 30, 1992

26 Rubottom, Wilbur—Interview, August 30, 1992

27 Rubottom, Wilbur—Interview, August 30, 1992

28 Haugen, Joe—Interview—June, 1992

29 Rubottom, Wilbur, Interview—August 30, 1992

30 Monzo, Judy—Interview—June, 1992

31 Green, Carol, Serra Statue Renovation—1986-1989

32 Minutes, Ventura City Council—1986-1989

33 *Ventura County Coast Reporter*—August 6, 1987, p.20

34 Burns, Russell—the Concrete Statue—Fr. Serra Statue— Nov. 16, 1988

35 Carol Green Files, Serra Statue Renovation

36 Author's visit to O.S.T. Grounds—July 23, 1992

37 Pfeiler, Robert—Interview, July 23, 1992

38 Green, Carol File—Serra Statue Renovation Kohl letter, Jan. 8, 1988

39 Rubottom, Wilbur, Interview, Sept. 1, 1992

40 Burns, Russell—Notes to Author (available at Ventura County Museum)

41 Rubottom, Wilbur, Interview—Sept. 1, 1992

42 Green, Carol, Serra Statue Renovation, 1986-1989

43 Kubilos, Charles, Interview, April 4, 1995

Catherine Antolino Mervyn

ABOUT THE AUTHOR

Catherine Antolino Mervyn is a native Italian who immigrated to America at the age of thirteen. She served in the U.S. Military for two years during WWII. Mrs. Mervyn received a B.S. degree in Education from Ohio State University and an M.A. degree in Education from California Lutheran University. She taught in elementary schools in Ohio, New Mexico and California. Her first book, *A Tower in the Valley,* The History of Santa Church was published in 1989, and **Historic Moments with California Federation of Women's Clubs** was published in 1998. Mrs. Mervyn and her husband live in Oxnard, CA.

www.ingramcontent.com/pod-product-compliance
Lightning Source LLC
Chambersburg PA
CBHW022105170526
45157CB00004B/1487